W9-APH-048

BARRON'S DOG BIBLES

Shih Tzu

Sharon Vanderlip, D.V.M.

Shih Tzu

Sharon Vanderlip, D.V.M.

Acknowledgments

I thank my husband, Jack Vanderlip, D.V.M., for his valuable help as expert veterinary consultant and evaluator. Thanks so much for taking care of our animals and a long list of home projects, so that I could have time to write this book. Thanks also to our daughter, Jacquelynn, for her smiles, help, and enthusiasm. These two wonderful people are the glue that holds me together! Finally, special thanks to Margery Squier of the Squier Group, and to Kim Guinn, of Sundown Shih Tzu, for their help and humor on a very hot day.

And last, this book is dedicated to the memory of Molly, a pretty little Shih Tzu that gave Helen 14 years of friendship and devotion.

About the Author

Sharon Vanderlip, D.V.M., has provided veterinary care to domestic and exotic animal species for 30 years. She has authored several books on dog breeds and animal care and published numerous articles for scientific, veterinary, and general reading audiences.

Dr. Vanderlip served as clinical veterinarian for the University of California San Diego School of Medicine and has collaborated on reproductive research projects with the Zoological Society of San Diego. She is former Chief of Veterinary Services for the National Aeronautics and Space Administration (NASA), and former Chief of Surgery for a large institution specializing in reproductive medicine.

Dr. Vanderlip has lectured at kennel clubs and veterinary associations worldwide on topics in canine and exotic animal medicine. She has received various awards for her writing and dedication to animal health.

Dr. Vanderlip may be contacted at *www.sharonvanderlip.com*

A Word About Pronouns

Many dog lovers feel that the pronoun "it" is not appropriate when referring to a pet that can be such a wonderful part of our lives. For this reason, Shih Tzu are described as "she" throughout this book unless the topic specifically relates to male dogs. This by no means infers any preference, nor should it be taken as an indication that either sex is particularly problematic.

Photo Credits

Photo Credits: Joan Balzarini: page 95; Kent Dannen: page 140; Tara Darling: pages 20, 33, 47, 66, 72, 80, 108, 129, 144, and 160; Jean Fogle: pages 120, 128, 154, and 159; Isabella Francais: pages 3, 7, 25, 26, 32, 40, 68, 74–75, 91, 110, 122, and 130; Curtis Hustace: page 56; Daniel Johnson/Paulette Johnson: pages 114–119; Paulette Johnson: pages vii, 10, 12, 14, 22–23, 29, 44, 48, 53–54, 60, 62–63, 73, 78, 104, 107, 109, 111, 112–113, 133–134, and 143; Margery Squier: pages 4, 9, 36, 50, 59, 64, 71, 76, 83, 93, 94, 99, 124, 149, and 150.

Cover Credits

Front cover and back cover: Shutterstock.

All inquiries should be addressed to:
Barron's Educational Series, Inc.
250 Wireless Boulevard
Hauppauge, New York 11788
www.barronseduc.com

ISBN-13 (book): 978-0-7641-6230-5
ISBN-10 (book): 0-7641-6230-6
ISBN-13 (DVD): 978-0-7641-8678-3
ISBN-10 (DVD): 0-7641-8678-7
ISBN-13 (package): 978-0-7641-9627-0
ISBN-10 (package): 0-7641-9627-8

Library of Congress Catalog Card No: 2008017012

Library of Congress Cataloging-in-Publication Data
Vanderlip, Sharon Lynn
  Shih tzu / by Sharon Vanderlip.
    p. cm.— (Barron's dog bibles)
  Includes index.
  ISBN-13: 978-0-7641-6230-5 (book)
  ISBN-10: 0-7641-6230-6 (book)
  ISBN-13: 978-0-7641-8678-3 (DVD)
  ISBN-10: 0-7641-8678-7 (DVD)
  ISBN-13: 978-0-7641-9627-0 (package)
  ISBN-10: 0-7641-9627-8 (package)
  [etc.]
1. Shih tzu. I. Title.

  SF429.S64V363 2009
  636.76—dc22

                    2008017012

Printed in China

9 8

CONTENTS

CONTENTS

The regal Shih Tzu is a descendent of some of the most ancient Asian breeds, including Tibetan "holy dogs" dating back more than 3,000 years. For centuries, these little "lion dogs" have been bred to be attractive, appealing, and affectionate. Shih Tzu have always been selected and raised for a very specific purpose: to be a constant devoted companion that is pampered, portable, beautiful, and highly prized. The Shih Tzu is all of that—and a lot more!

The Shih Tzu has a magical ability to attract admirers and win their love in a heartbeat. So it is not surprising that this bright little toy breed with the glorious coat has now drawn your attention, too! There are many reasons why the Shih Tzu has such a powerful, magnetic appeal. When we see a little Shih Tzu, we respond in a big way. Part of this is because of the Shih Tzu's overwhelming charm—and part of this is because of who we are, and what we seek, need, and desire in a canine companion. In fact, the more we learn about the Shih Tzu, the greater our desire to own and care for one—and the more we learn about ourselves.

At first, you are attracted to the Shih Tzu's unique physical features. But spend a little time with a Shih Tzu and you soon learn that the true treasure lies deeper, in the complex workings of the Shih Tzu's mind: her extreme devotion and desire to please; her response to human emotions, words, and signals; her intelligence and learning ability; her keen sensitivity to your moods. In some ways, a Shih Tzu seems eerily almost human. This is not surprising. For centuries the Shih Tzu was bred specifically to be a devoted, affectionate, and constant companion for humans; with a physical appearance that is appealing by all standards in all cultures. The Shih Tzu is finely tuned to observe and respond to human behaviors and emotions. This is a large component of the Shih Tzu's "mystique."

It is not by chance that the Shih Tzu ranks among the most popular breeds in the world. And it is not a coincidence that throughout its long history, Shih Tzu have stolen the hearts of thousands of people worldwide, including royalty, dignitaries, religious leaders, and celebrities. This toy breed is the successful result of centuries of human intervention and intense selection, in an effort to develop a dog with a unique appearance, a special purpose, and enormous appeal. The Shih Tzu is, in a word, exquisite.

Whether you already own a Shih Tzu, or you are considering adding one to your life, this book gives you the valuable information you need to understand your Shih Tzu and her innate behaviors. This book will help you give your Shih Tzu the very best of care and ensure that she is well socialized, emotionally balanced, healthy, and happy throughout her life.

Sharon Vanderlip, D.V.M.

Chapter One

All About Shih Tzu

History tells us that Shih Tzu were originally bred to resemble small lions, so when we examine a Shih Tzu, we admire the dedicated efforts of the earliest breeders, as well as their vivid imaginations. It is obvious that early Shih Tzu breeders' selections were also greatly influenced by something very basic: human evolutionary adaptation and the "nurturing response" (sometimes called the "cute response"). When we first see a Shih Tzu, words like "cute" quickly spring to mind. We all know and recognize this natural response. It is an arcane facet of human nature and it is responsible for some of the Shih Tzu's enormous worldwide popularity. How?

In 1949, Dr. Konrad Lorenz, the famous zoologist/psychologist/ornithologist, theorized that infantile, or baby-like, features triggered a "nurturing response" in adults and that it was this innate response that made adults take care of babies and ensured species survival. Studies have since shown that this human nurturing response also crosses over to animals. Humans react in a strong, positive, instinctive way to animals that retain baby-like features, such as a large round head, large eyes, small nose, and a small body. (Small bodies trigger the nurturing response because they are associated with helplessness, innocence, affection, and nonaggressive behavior.) We think animals with infantile features are "cute" and we naturally want to hold them, feed them, and take care of them.

Everyone agrees that Shih Tzu, especially Shih Tzu puppies, are very cute. In fact, their "cuteness" has, in many ways, caused serious problems for Shih Tzu because of impulse buyers and puppy mills. As cute and wonderful as they are, Shih Tzu are not suitable pets for everyone. There is a lot to know about this beautiful and extraordinary breed before deciding to embark on the very big, long-term commitment of Shih Tzu ownership. Shih Tzu require a lot of care and attention, must live indoors, need frequent grooming, have special needs, and live a long time. Shih Tzu bond closely with their owners and thrive on human companionship. Being a responsible, dedicated owner means spending as much time as possible with your Shih Tzu, for many years, and learning as much as you can about the breed. It also entails a significant financial obligation and commitment.

A Brief History

The Shih Tzu's sweet appearance and gentle demeanor belie that fact that this toy breed is actually a twig on a huge and partly ferocious family tree with deep, primitive roots. Like every dog breed in existence today, the Shih Tzu traces back to Hesperocyonines, a prehistoric carnivorous animal that evolved in North America about 40 million years ago. Hesperocyonines resembled a cross between a weasel and a fox and gave rise to several canine species before its extinction 15 million years ago. The Shih Tzu's early ancestors migrated to Asia about seven million years ago, presumably by way of a land bridge in existence at that time.

Shih Tzu are brachycephalic dogs: dogs that have short, rounded skulls, flat faces, and short noses. Shih Tzu, and many other Asiatic breeds, were selected specifically for their brachycephalic characteristics and were deliberately bred with the original intention of producing a type of dog that was supposed to resemble a miniature lion. Lions held special religious significance among Buddhists, and were considered Buddha's sacred and most important beast. Lions are not native to Asia and were difficult to keep in captivity centuries ago. So it is not surprising that great effort went into creating dogs that, in the imaginative eyes of their breeders and owners, resembled diminutive lions. "Lion dogs," also known as "royal dogs," were said to bring good luck, house the souls of lamas, contain the spirits of Buddhist monks, and to follow in Buddha's footsteps. "Lion dogs" were even credited with the ability to transform into a real lion. These rare and remarkable little dogs were so highly treasured that they were sometimes given as gifts to emperors and dignitaries, included in royal processions, in works of art, on tapestries, and painted in imperial books. "Lion dogs" could be given as gifts, but historians report that selling a "lion dog" was considered a crime punishable by death.

Shih Tzu Through the Centuries

There has been much speculation about which breeds formed the foundation of the Shih Tzu breed. Some people think that Lhasa Apsos were crossed with Pekingese. Others think that the Tibetan Spaniel was bred with the Pekingese to create a predecessor of the Shih Tzu. Two things are certain: 1) The Shih Tzu is the result of interbreeding original Tibetan "holy dogs" and various "lion dogs" in China; and 2) The Shih Tzu's ancestors are the oldest and smallest of the Tibetan "holy dogs," dating back more than 3,000 years.

It is unknown when the Shih Tzu's ancestors first reached China from Tibet. Estimated times range from as early as 618 C.E. to as late as the nineteenth century, but because accurate records were not always kept, or were lost, historians cannot be sure.

Some researchers state that around 1653 the Dalai Lama visited China and brought three "holy dogs," or "Tibetan lion dogs," with him as gifts for the Emperor. Many Shih Tzu experts believe that these three dogs were bred with Pekingese dogs in a continuing effort to create ideal "lion dogs" and that these animals, along with the probable introduction of Pugs and other small Asiatic breeds 150 years later, are the likely ancestors of today's Shih Tzu. Unfortunately, civil unrest, war, and invasions eliminated "lion dogs" from Tibet and by 1750, they could only be found in the imperial palace in Peking (Beijing).

Historians report that in 1908 the 13th Dalai Lama gave the dowager empress of China (T'Zu Hsi) several Shih Tzu-type dogs (Tibetan lion dogs) while he was in Peking, after he fled the British invasion of Tibet. Despite being a cruel and ruthless ruler, the empress cherished her little dogs and took a special interest in them. She kept her Shih Tzu, Pekingese, and Pugs separate and was instrumental in the development of the Shih Tzu breed.

When the empress died in late 1908, some of her dogs were obtained by wealthy individuals or given as gifts to dignitaries. China eventually formed a kennel club in 1923 and a few Shih Tzu were imported into the United Kingdom in the 1930s. Unfortunately, the China Kennel Club neglected to create a registry or write a breed standard or description for the Shih Tzu until 1938,

Breed Truths

In addition to the Shih Tzu, many Asiatic breeds were bred to resemble small lions, including the Lhasa Apso, Pug, and Japanese Chin.

making judging and breeding to a specific type difficult.

In 1949, the Communists invaded Peking (Beijing) and dog breeding in China came to an abrupt end. Fortunately, through the dedicated efforts of a few Shih Tzu enthusiasts, particularly in the United Kingdom, the breed was saved from extinction.

Shih Tzu Around the World

During the early 1900s, Shih Tzu were occasionally imported into Europe by diplomats or British admiralty who had been stationed in China. Not all imported Shih Tzu had complete pedigrees and not all of them were used for breeding. In fact, the Shih Tzu had so many different names at the time, and the written standard for them was so recent, and records so incomplete, that breed purity or authenticity was sometimes questioned. It is important to keep in mind that these few animals were all that remained of the Shih Tzu breed and the Shih Tzu's ancient lineage. If they had not safely escaped China, or had not been saved through importation, you would not have your little lion dog today. From the 1930s on, the future of the Shih Tzu breed depended entirely on breeders in the United Kingdom, other parts of Europe, and North America. It is because of their efforts that the Shih Tzu breed was saved from extinction.

Only fourteen dogs make up the foundation of all Shih Tzu in existence today.

England When Shih Tzu were first imported to England, they were called Tibetan Lion Dogs or Apsos and were exhibited in the same class with Lhasa Apsos (known at that time as Tibetan Apsos). Eventually the Kennel Club recognized that Shih Tzu and Lhasa Apsos were two different breeds with very distinctive traits (Lhasa Apsos not only look different from Shih Tzu, but their personalities are also quite different).

In 1934, a Shih Tzu club was formed and the breed's popularity blossomed. Even Queen Elizabeth took a special interest in Shih Tzu, which naturally added to

Fun Facts

Shih Tzu were called the "chrysanthemum-faced dog" because of the way the hairs on the flat, round face grow outward—similar to the petals of a chrysanthemum flower.

the public's growing attraction to this new, exotic import.

The Earl of Essex imported Tashi of Chouette from Canada in 1938. Lieutenant General Telfer-Smollett, Lord Lieutenant of Dunbartonshire imported Ming, a black and white female. The lieutenant also imported Ishuh Tzu, a gray and white female, in 1948.

By 1939, the British Kennel Club had registered 183 Shih Tzu. But scarcely had the Shih Tzu recovered in small numbers, when it was once again teetering on the edge of extinction—and once again because of the tragedy of war. The onset of World War II brought all breeding, exhibiting, competing, and importing of dogs to a rapid halt. Between 1940 and 1947 there were only 61 Shih Tzu in the United Kingdom and of these, only two were newly registered (in 1945) with the Kennel Club of England.

Mr. and Mrs. Buchanon imported Wuffles, a gold male, in 1948 and Mr. and Mrs. Morris imported Mai-ting, a black and white female of unknown pedigree, in 1949.

Finally, in 1952, the last Shih Tzu to leave China, a yellow and white female named Hsi-Li-Ya, was imported by Mr. R.P. Dobson. Hsi-Li-Ya escaped China just before the Communist Revolution that led to the extermination of many dog breeds in Asia.

Ireland On the Emerald Isle, Miss E. Madeleine Hutchins was among the first to import and breed Shih Tzu. Her 1930 import, a black and white dog of unknown parentage, named Lung-fu-ssu, is one of the fourteen ancestors behind today's Shih Tzu.

Norway In 1932, Mrs. Henrik Kauffman imported three Shih Tzu to Norway: Aido, a black and white male; Leidza, a gold or brown female; and Schauder, a black and white female. These three dogs were the first Shih Tzu ever imported into Scandinavia.

Thirteen of the foundation Shih Tzu are discussed above, but what about the 14th? The story of Philadelphus Suti-T-sun of Elfann is a special one, because although

Breed Truths

The white blaze on a Shih Tzu's forehead is sometimes called the "star of Buddha" and the dark markings on a Shih Tzu's back are referred to as Buddha's saddle.

most Shih Tzu alive today are related to him, he was not a Shih Tzu at all. He was a Pekingese. What happened?

When World War II ended, there were very few Shih Tzu left in the world. There were no Shih Tzu remaining in China. Many Shih Tzu had health problems or died at an early age. The Shih Tzu gene pool was very small and breeders were understandably concerned that some problems might be hereditary. Breeders feared that without genetic diversity, the breed could risk becoming too inbred and be lost.

Fun Facts

The Shih Tzu was used as the informal symbol in 1994 for the Chinese Year of the Dog.

Breeders decided to breed as many of the remaining Shih Tzu as possible and not remove any animal from the breeding program just because it had a minor flaw. As a result of these breeding efforts, the Shih Tzu increased in size and weight and became larger than the original Shih Tzu from China.

In 1952, Elfreda Evans, a dog fancier relatively new to the Shih Tzu community, did the unthinkable. She deliberately bred a Shih Tzu to a Pekingese. Mrs. Evans believed her actions were justified because the Shih Tzu population and gene pool were small. She thought Shih Tzu were too inbred. Mrs. Evans believed that by crossing a Shih Tzu with a Pekingese (a breed that many people believed had already been crossed with Shih Tzu in earlier times) she could reduce the size of the Shih Tzu and improve bone structure and the muzzle. (Size continued to be a concern years after Mrs. Evans' controversial breeding program and in 1962 the Manchu Shih Tzu Society began efforts to reduce the size of the Shih Tzu back to its original weight of 10 pounds—the original size of Shih Tzu housed in the Imperial Palace.)

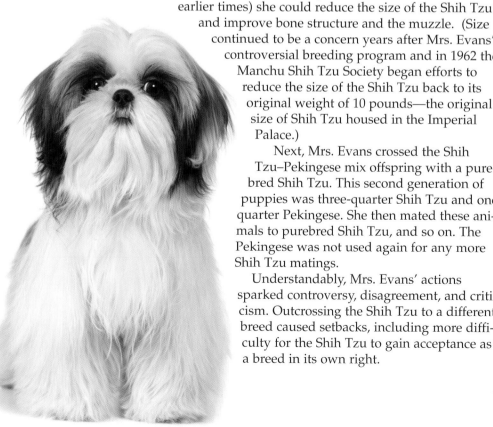

Next, Mrs. Evans crossed the Shih Tzu–Pekingese mix offspring with a purebred Shih Tzu. This second generation of puppies was three-quarter Shih Tzu and one-quarter Pekingese. She then mated these animals to purebred Shih Tzu, and so on. The Pekingese was not used again for any more Shih Tzu matings.

Understandably, Mrs. Evans' actions sparked controversy, disagreement, and criticism. Outcrossing the Shih Tzu to a different breed caused setbacks, including more difficulty for the Shih Tzu to gain acceptance as a breed in its own right.

Shih Tzu that were descendents of the Shih Tzu–Pekingese cross were recorded as such in the Kennel Club records. The Kennel Club did not recognize any of the descendents of the Shih Tzu–Pekingese outcross as "purebred" Shih Tzu until they were at least four generations removed from the original Shih Tzu–Pekingese mating. **Note:** In the United States the AKC requirement was more strict, being six generations removed.

By 1966, there were 15 registered Shih Tzu champions in the United Kingdom that were descendents from Mrs. Evans' Shih Tzu–Pekingese cross. Although her Pekingese is one of the 14 foundation animals of the today's Shih Tzu breed, not all Shih Tzu are descendents of the Pekingese outcross. Other breeders chose to limit their breedings to Shih Tzu only, no matter how limited the gene pool was. Unfortunately, descendents from these pure Shih Tzu lines are rare today.

Shih Tzu populations, clubs, and shows are now well-established throughout most of the world. Shih Tzu are especially popular in the United States, Europe, Australia, South Africa, Latin America, and Japan.

Breed Truths

Because of wars and revolutions, Shih Tzu were eliminated in Asia and all dog breeding essentially ceased by the early 1900s. In contrast, dog breeding in the United States and Europe gained in popularity and the American Kennel Club was formed in 1884. Thousands of dogs were registered with the AKC by the late nineteenth century, but not one of them was a Shih Tzu. Today, Shih Tzu rank among the ten most popular dogs in the United States and rank fifth as the breed with the greatest number of AKC annual litter registrations.

Shih Tzu Come to America

In 1938, Shih Tzu came to the United States. A few Shih Tzu were imported from China, but most of those animals had only one generation pedigrees (only the parents were known). Most of the first Shih Tzu imports were brought to the United States by military personnel who had been stationed in the United Kingom during World War II. Throughout the 1950s, Americans continued to purchase and import their Shih Tzu from U.K. breeders.

Shih Tzu enthusiasts formed a breed club in 1938, but it was a long time before Shih Tzu received American Kennel Club (AKC) breed recognition. Initially, Shih Tzu could only be listed as, and exhibited with, Lhasa Apsos. The AKC finally acknowledged the Shih Tzu as a distinct breed in 1955 and listed it as a member of the Miscellaneous Class. This allowed Shih Tzu to compete for awards in obedience trials but did not allow them to compete in conformation (beauty according to a set standard) classes.

Shih Tzu breeders worked hard to achieve AKC recognition for their dogs. By 1960, there were three Shih Tzu clubs: the Texas Shih Tzu Society, the Shih Tzu Club of America, and the American Shih Tzu Association. In 1963, the Texas Shih Tzu Society and the Shih Tzu Club of America united to form the American Shih Tzu Club (ASTC). By 1964, there were approximately 400 Shih Tzu registered in the United States.

Although Shih Tzu fanciers made a lot of progress, they still faced challenges in their breeding programs. China had no more animals to export and the AKC would not register any Shih Tzu that was not at least six generations removed from Mrs. Evans' 1952 Shih Tzu–Pekingese cross. Finally, in March 1969, the AKC admitted Shih Tzu for registration in the AKC Stud Book, and to regular show classification in the Toy Group at AKC shows on September 1, 1969. That same September day, Shih Tzu Champion Chumulari Ying-Ying

Breed Truths

The Shih Tzu has had many names throughout its long history. The breed was not referred to as a Shih Tzu until about the late fourteenth century. Other names for Shih Tzu and their ancestors are

- Lion dog
- Holy dog
- Royal dog
- Fu dog
- Foo dog
- Chrysanthemum-faced dog
- Under the table dog
- Shih Tzu Kou
- Lhasa Lion Dog
- Lhasa Terrier
- Long-haired lion dog
- Ha-Pa'rh Kou
- Tibetan holy dog
- Tibetan lion dog
- Tibetan Poodle
- Tibetan temple dog
- Tribute dog
- Shock Dog
- Apso

won Best in Show in New Jersey against 970 other dogs, and his father, Champion Bjorneholms Pif, won the Toy Group in Illinois. At the same time, Lakoya Princess Tanya Shu won the Toy Group in Oregon.

From the time the first Shih Tzu club formed, to the time the breed was finally admitted for AKC registration, breeders spent 38 years promoting the Shih Tzu and working hard for breed recognition. Then, suddenly, Shih Tzu took the show scene by storm and became an overnight sensation. Show victories were numerous and championship titles were earned in record time. The Shih Tzu's popularity soared and with it, so did its numbers. In 1969 the AKC registered approximately 3,000 Shih Tzu, and 100 Shih Tzu earned their championship titles in 1970. The Shih Tzu had won titles, trophies, and a permanent place in America's heart!

Ten years later, in 1980, the Shih Tzu population numbered in the thousands and in 1989 the ASTC created a more descriptive standard for the breed.

According to AKC statistics, the Shih Tzu now ranks among the ten most popular breeds and Shih Tzu litter registrations rank fifth highest (out of more than 150 AKC recognized breeds). The AKC registers an astounding 30,000 to 40,000 Shih Tzu annually.

Breed Truths

One of the greatest moments in Shih Tzu history was when Champion Ellingham Kala Nag won Best of Breed at Crufts in 1963. The exotic Asian breed with the long and turbulent history had survived all odds. The Shih Tzu was well on its way to winning championships—and hearts—around the world.

Shih Tzu Characteristics

A Shih Tzu is first and foremost a companion, so her character and personality are extremely important. In fact, Shih Tzu temperament is such an important consideration in the breed that it is included and described in the official AKC standard.

Shih Tzu should be confident, outgoing, happy, friendly, affectionate, and trusting. They should never by nervous, shy, or aggressive. A Shih Tzu should be bright, alert, and lively. She should move in a proud, arrogant, aristocratic manner with her head held high and her tail curved over her back.

Shih Tzu Standard

The Shih Tzu is a compact, solid, sturdy dog. Shih Tzu should be low to the ground, but never appear squatty. A well-balanced Shih Tzu is slightly longer than she is tall.

One of the most distinguishing features of the Shih Tzu is the round, broad, domed head. There should be a generous space between the eyes. A narrow head or close-set eye placement is a fault in the breed because they detract from the Shih Tzu's soft, sweet expression. A beautiful Shih Tzu always has a wide-eyed, friendly, and trusting appearance. Large, expressive, round, dark eyes are preferred.

The muzzle should have a definite stop and be set no lower than the bottom eyelids. The muzzle is square, unwrinkled, and short. Ideally the muzzle is no longer than 1 inch (2.54 cm) from the tip of the nose to the stop (larger dogs may have slightly longer muzzles). The broad nostrils are wide and open, not pinched shut. Ears are large and heavily coated and set slightly below the crown of the skull. The Shih Tzu's jaw is broad and wide and the lips should meet evenly. The teeth and tongue should not be visible when the mouth is closed. A missing tooth or slightly misaligned teeth are not uncommon.

The Shih Tzu is an aristocratic, noble dog with a well-balanced appearance. The neck should be long enough to allow the dog to carry her head high and to be in balance with her height and body length. The body should be sturdy and the back (topline) should be level. The chest is deep with well-sprung ribs. The tail is set high, heavily plumed (covered with lots of long, thick hair) and carried over the back, like a "teapot handle." Shih Tzu legs are straight, strong, and well-muscled. Short hocks provide greater drive in the hindquarters. Feet should point straight ahead. Dewclaw removal is optional.

Movement, or gait, is extremely important in the Shih Tzu and should appear smooth, effortless, and flowing. The graceful, fluid gait of the Shih Tzu is emphasized by a beautiful, properly groomed, flowing coat.

Size Size ranges from 9 to $10^1/2$ inches at the shoulders, females usually being smaller than males. Shih Tzu should not be taller than 11 inches or shorter than 8 inches. Ideal weight is from 9 to 16 pounds and should be in proportion to the animal.

Shih Tzu Colors

Shih Tzu come in a variety of colors and markings, ranging from golden to black. All colors are permissible and no color is considered more desirable than another. **Note:** Some Shih Tzu coat colors may change as the animal ages. The coat should be luxurious, dense, double-coated, long, and flowing. Hair should not be curly, but a slight wave to the coat is permissible. The following is a list of the Shih Tzu colors.

- Gold
- Gold and white
- Cream
- Deep red
- Red and white
- Grizzle gray
- Silver and white
- Brindle
- Liver
- Blue
- Black-masked
- Black tips
- Solid black
- Black and white
- Saddle markings
- White blaze

Note: Nose, lips, and eyelid margins must be black and eyes should be dark unless the animal is liver or blue colored, in which case the pigmentation must complement the coat color.

Chapter Two

The Mind of a Shih Tzu

Your Shih Tzu looks at you intently. She seems to be studying your facial features for signs of emotion as she closely watches your every move. She listens attentively to your voice intonations and words. At times your Shih Tzu acts like she is almost human. She behaves as though she understands every word you say. Sometimes it seems like she can almost read your mind!

Just what *is* your Shih Tzu thinking? How much does she reason? What goes on inside that pretty little head? Why does your Shih Tzu want and seek out your constant companionship? Why does she behave the way she does? And just how much of what *you think* your Shih Tzu is thinking is really part of her thought processes and innate behavior—and how much is actually due to your own projections and how you think, act, stimulate, and interpret her behavior and responses?

We often attribute Shih Tzu with many characteristics that are uniquely human. This is called anthropomorphism, from the Greek words *anthropose* (human) and *morphe* (shape, form). When we consider an animal in this way, we also treat it more like a little person, than like an animal. This treatment in turn affects the way the animal behaves and responds to us, and their responses further enforce the manner in which we treat them, as well as our perception of them as being human-like.

No matter how smart your Shih Tzu is and how human-like she seems, she is, after all, a dog. By understanding and taking advantage of your Shih Tzu's innate *dog* behaviors, and keeping your expectations reasonable, you can teach your Shih Tzu to be a well-socialized, well-mannered, and well-adjusted canine citizen.

Shih Tzu Personality

The Shih Tzu's mind is a combination of innate engrained behaviors, emotions, memories, perceptions, genetics, and acquired and reinforced behaviors. These are influenced by a variety of factors, especially the manner in which the Shih Tzu is raised, socialized, and trained. The animal's experiences and her environment also play a big role in how she thinks and behaves. For example, the first 12 weeks of a Shih Tzu's life are the most critical and

13

impressionable when it comes to person-ality development, especially between the ages of three and nine weeks of age. Some of a Shih Tzu's behavior is instinctive, but the breed has been so highly domesticated for so many centuries, that a great deal more of her personality and behavior is influenced by humans, experiences, and environment, than by the genetics of her ancient ancestors.

Shih Tzu Senses

Shih Tzu have very keen senses, espe-cially when compared with humans. Yet, compared with breeds that have strongly relied on their senses for survival for cen-turies, some Shih Tzu's senses may not be as keen. For example, through genera-tions of selective breeding some Shih Tzu senses have been mildly compromised because of the development of desired physical traits.

Sense of Smell

Shih Tzu have a keen sense of smell, especially when compared with humans, but because they are brachy-cephalic (flat-faced with a short nose), there is less space for olfactory recep-tor cells in a Shih Tzu's snout than in a breed with a longer muzzle. A Shih Tzu's sense of smell is equipped with several million olfactory receptor cells, yet it cannot come close to the olfactory senses of a Bloodhound or a wolf, which has more than 200 million olfactory receptor cells. Nevertheless, compared to humans, who have about 5 million olfactory receptor cells, a Shih Tzu's sense of smell is extraordinary. In fact, a Shih Tzu's olfactory center is about 40 times larger than a human's and her sense of smell is esti-mated to be one million times more efficient than that of a human.

Breed Truths

The Shih Tzu's Asian ancestors were the most ancient of domesticated breeds, making the Shih Tzu's line-age one of the oldest breeds in existence today. When most dogs were still wild hunters with strong wolf-like instincts and behaviors, the Shih Tzu was already sitting on laps—closely and irrevocably bonded with humans and living in their homes. Shih Tzu are extremely people-oriented dogs and are entirely dependent upon humans for their care, survival, and propa-gation. Shih Tzu still retain some of their ancestors' primitive instincts, but many of those instincts are buried in the recesses of the Shih Tzu's mind, and tend to surface more often during fearful or stress-ful situations.

PERSONALITY POINTERS

Shih Tzu Personality

Normal Shih Tzu Personality	Shih Tzu Problem Behavior
Playful	Fearful
Outgoing	Shy
Inquisitive	Reclusive
Affectionate	Runs when approached
Sweet	Growls without provocation
Arrogant	Aggressive
Sometimes bossy	Nips with intent to harm
Easily spoiled	Fear-biter
Show off	Incompatible with littermates
Interested in new sights and sounds and investigates	Struggles to escape when picked up
	Yelps or protests when held
Approaches in greeting	Does not enjoy human company
Loves to be with people	Does not want to be pet
Loves to be picked up, carried, cuddled, and pampered	Is not eager to please

Sense of Taste

Like all dogs, the Shih Tzu's sense of taste is closely linked to sense of smell. Dogs have fewer taste buds than humans (about 1,700 buds compared to approximately 9,000 taste buds in humans) and most dogs' taste buds are clustered near the tip of the tongue. In addition, dogs have a vomeronasal organ at the roof of their mouths. This organ enables dogs to "taste" smells and sends the sensory information to the limbic system of the brain, which is responsible for many emotional responses. In other words, much of a Shih Tzu's sense of food enjoyment seems to be because of the way the food smells, rather than how it tastes. This helps explain why some dogs eat strange things that might not be good or safe for them, such as foreign objects, or aluminum foil that was used to wrap food.

Breed Truths

When they were housed in monasteries and palaces, Shih Tzu duties included "guarding" and barking warning alerts at the approach of strangers or danger. Shih Tzu still take this job seriously. They make good watchdogs and will bark to alert their families to possible threats.

When Good Dogs Behave Badly

A bored dog can get into mischief and that's when good dogs do bad things. With nothing to entertain them, puppies and adult dogs become bored and find trouble. They may chew and destroy objects, bark incessantly, and urinate and defecate in the house. Here are some ways to help your dog avoid boredom:

- Play with your puppy often and spend lots of time with her every day. Shih Tzu were bred to be constant companions, so it is not surprising that they can develop behavior problems when they are isolated from their people for too long. Shih Tzu are not the kind of dog that can be left alone or ignored for extended periods of time. If you don't have *a lot* of time for a Shih Tzu, don't get one!
- Give your Shih Tzu the exercise she needs and take her on walks and outings at least three times a day.
- Provide your Shih Tzu with mental stimulation such as fun games and interesting toys: indestructible rubber toys to chew; treat-filled toys; and toys to chase or drag.
- Use simple games as fun training methods.
- Teach, train, and review simple tricks and commands, such as following you or coming to you when called and praise and reward your Shih Tzu for a good performance.
- Use positive reinforcement and reward your Shih Tzu with lots of praise and affection, and an occasional food reward, whenever she is good. *Never give praise or a food reward for undesirable behavior.*

Sight

Shih Tzu see well, but because they were not bred for hunting and do not rely heavily on vision for survival, Shih Tzu are near-sighted and their vision is not as keen as that of some other breeds, such as sight hounds. Shih Tzu may also have hereditary eye problems that can interfere with sight.

Hearing

Shih Tzu have a keen sense of hearing. Human hearing range is 20 Hz to 20 kHz (the higher range is usually noted only in young people who do not have ear damage or disease). Shih Tzu hearing range is about 67 Hz to 45 kHz, enabling Shih Tzu to hear higher frequencies than humans can hear. But Shih Tzu do not hear as well as dogs with erect ears, such as German Shepherds or Basenjis. These animals have the advantage of being able to increase or decrease the intensity of a sound reaching their ears simply by directing their pinnae (ear flap) toward, or away from, the source of the sound. Your Shih Tzu will move her ears instinctively to try to capture sound, but the heavily coated pendulous ears that cover the ear canals block and soften some sounds.

Sense of Touch

Shih Tzu have delicate skin and are sensitive to touch. They have been bred specifically to be caressed and cuddled and to enjoy human touch and affection. Shih Tzu need frequent grooming, so care must be taken not to injure or traumatize your dog's sensitive skin. The way you handle your Shih Tzu is very important, as she relies on your hands as an important form of communication. Your hands should not inflict pain or discomfort.

Body Language

In most breeds, body language is more obvious than in the Shih Tzu. For example, when dogs are anxious, they sometimes narrow their eyes, but because of the size and shape of a Shih Tzu's eyes, eye sockets, and lids, their eyes usually remain wide open. Sometimes the sclera (the white part of the eye surrounding the colored iris) becomes more noticeable when the

PERSONALITY POINTERS
Shih Tzu Body Language

Shih Tzu Mood	Friendly	Curious or Excited	Playful
Head Carriage	Normal posture and head position	Normal posture and head position	"Play bow," chest and head lowered to ground, head looking up
Eyes	Wide open	Wide open	Wide open
Ears	Alert, forward	Alert, forward	Alert, forward
Mouth	Closed or relaxed and slightly open in a "smile"	Mouth open, teeth covered with lips, may pant	Closed or slightly open
Body	Relaxed posture or wiggling with excitement	Very still and observant, or very animated	Chest lowered to ground, rump elevated
Tail	Wagging	Wagging	Wagging

Shih Tzu is frightened. Additionally, dogs drop their tails when they are frightened or submissive; however, Shih Tzu naturally carry their tails high, curled over their backs, and their tails are heavily coated, so a change in tail carriage is not always immediately obvious. Finally, dogs show pilo-erection (hair standing out straight from the body, or looking fluffy to make the animal look larger) along their neck, shoulder blades, and back when they are agitated. Pilo-erection is difficult to detect on a Shih Tzu because of coat type and length.

Face and Mouth Signals
Your Shih Tzu has fewer facial expressions than you do, because dogs have less small facial muscles than humans. Nevertheless, dogs use their face and mouths to communicate. When your Shih Tzu's facial muscles are relaxed and her mouth is wide open, it means she feels no tension or conflict. If your Shih Tzu acts as though she is "kissing" you, by trying to lick at the corners of your mouth, she is not really "kissing." She is trying to get food information. Puppies instinctively nuzzle at their mother's mouth so she will open it and share food in her mouth (or regurgitated food) with them.

Apprehensive or Anxious	Fearful	Subordinate
Neck stiff, head may be pulled back slightly	Head slightly lowered	Head slightly lowered
Wide open, may appear "bug-eyed," whites of eyes may show, may have fixed stare	Eyes wide, whites of eyes may show	Eyes partially closed
Pulled back	Ears pulled back or flattened against skull	Ears flattened against skull
Closed or slightly open in a tight "grin" with teeth showing	Slightly open, teeth may be visible, may be drooling	Lips of mouth pulled back in "grin," may lick or nuzzle
Tense	Tense, trembling, may take up on a position poised to run, may release anal sac contents in fear	May roll over on back and expose belly, may also dribble urine in submission
Partially lowered	Lowered, between legs	Lowered, between legs

Behavior Problems

Behavior problems develop because people do not spend enough time with their dogs, do not adequately socialize them, and do not properly train them. People also tend to inadvertently reinforce a dog's undesirable behavior by sending mixed messages about acceptable behavior and confusing the animal. As most people are not professional dog trainers or animal therapists, owners trying to correct behaviors on their own can make the situation worse. Sadly, for most dogs the undesirable behaviors are usually well-established and difficult to change by the time an expert is consulted.

One of the most common mistakes people make is allowing misbehavior to continue

Helpful Hints

Some dogs bark because they are in pain, or because they have cognitive dysfunction (senility). They may also be responding to sounds that humans cannot hear. If you cannot stop or modify your dog's barking, consult a veterinarian to be certain there are no underlying causes for the behavior.

19

until it becomes a habit, or refusing to take immediate, necessary, and effective disciplinary actions, such as a distraction, "time out," or crate training. By not taking immediate action to correct the behavior, it sends the wrong message to the dog that the behavior is acceptable and reinforces the undesirable behavior.

Preventing behavior problems, through early and appropriate socialization and training, is much easier than modifying undesirable behaviors.

Four key steps to behavior modification and avoiding mixed messages are

- Do not reward undesirable behavior.
- Distract from the bad behavior (you can use a toy as a distraction to change the behavior).

- Encourage good behavior (for example, call your Shih Tzu to you and ask her to sit).
- Reward good behavior only (when your dog stops her bad behavior, responds to you and does what you asked her to do, give her a food reward or lots of praise).

Dealing with Fears

There are many ways owners unintentionally reinforce their dogs' fears and undesirable behaviors by sending mixed messages. One of the most common and serious mistakes is to baby or coddle a dog, speak to it in babytalk, and behave protectively (such as clutching the dog close to your chest) when the animal acts shy or frightened. This is especially true if the dog is frightened about things that are commonplace, routinely encountered in everyday life, and not threatening. When an owner behaves in this manner, the dog interprets this to mean that there is, indeed, something to fear. The animal also associates fear behavior with receiving extra attention and affection. In essence, fear behavior is being reinforced and rewarded.

Most fears can be prevented through socialization and training early in life. Shyness is a serious character flaw in a Shih Tzu. Your Shih Tzu should be confident and outgoing. If she exhibits fear behavior, do not overreact and do not behave as though her fears are justified or real. Distract her attention from the perceived threat by calling her to you and asking her to do something, such as *sit*, and then reward her for her good, calm, fearless behavior. Continue to increase your Shih Tzu's social experiences in "baby steps" and make sure they are all positive. Introduce her to new situations and people and reward her for calm, confident, behavior.

CAUTION

Medications for Behavioral Modification

In today's world we often try to address many of our behavioral and emotional problems with medications. We do this for ourselves and for our children—and recently we have begun to do this for our pets. Preventing behavior problems is better and easier than treating them. Behavior problems can be prevented through early and positive socialization and training. The second best thing is to address the pets' problems by customized socialization and training, depending on the behavioral problem(s), whenever possible. Medications should be considered as a last resort for difficult cases in which the dog's behavior, fears, phobias, and anxieties do not respond to training and socialization alone, and are making life miserable for the animal and the owner.

Dealing with Barking

Many Shih Tzu make good watch dogs. They bark an alert if a stranger approaches or danger is near. But some dogs bark at everyone and everything, because they have not been taught that it is wrong, or because they have been isolated and are lonely. They do not know what is acceptable to bark at (such as a stranger breaking into the house) and what is not acceptable (such as barking for no apparent reason, or to get attention or affection). Even worse, some dogs don't know when to *stop* barking.

CAUTION

Some Shih Tzu suffer from congenital (present at birth) deafness. It is very important to have your Shih Tzu's hearing tested if your Shih Tzu ignores you or acts like she does not hear you; does not come when called; is startled when people or animals approach; is shy or easily frightened or confused. Contact your veterinarian for a referral to a veterinary college or veterinary neurologist.

Owners often make a common mistake when they try to teach their dogs to stop barking. They join in the chaos by shouting at their dog to "Be quiet," or "Stop that!" Owners who shout at their dogs are only sending mixed messages that confuse the dog. When people shout, the dog responds as though there is a valid reason for barking. The dog interprets the owner's shouting and behavior as joining in on the noise-making. This reinforces the dog's idea that there must be "something to shout (or bark) about," and reinforces undesirable behavior.

If there is a way to eliminate the cause or stimulus for barking, then do so. For example, if your dog barks at a specific item, such as a yard sprinkler, then bring your dog inside when the sprinklers are running.

Sometimes you can anticipate that your dog will bark before she does. In these situations, distract your Shih Tzu *before* she barks, call her to you, ask her to sit or down, then praise her. The more often you can prevent the bad habit, the faster you can modify your dog's behavior.

For additional training, take your Shih Tzu different places where she can meet people, hear new sounds, and have new experiences. If she barks for no apparent reason, then distract her, call her, ask her to sit, and then praise her for being calm and quiet.

Of course, if your Shih Tzu barks for a good reason, such as smoke in the house, or an attempted burglary, you would naturally reward her for her courageous behavior!

Dealing with Chewing

Puppies investigate with their mouths and have a natural urge and need to chew, especially during the teething period, when teeth are erupting and gums are sore. Dogs enjoy chewing and all dogs should be given safe, indestructible chew toys for their well-being and entertainment. Avoid mixed messages: Puppies must be taught early on which items they are allowed to chew. Teach your Shih Tzu that she can only chew on safe chew toys that you give her. Do not give your puppy something inappropriate to chew, such as an old

FYI: Dealing with Separation Anxiety

Separation anxiety cases make up 19 percent of canine problem behavior cases referred to veterinary behavior specialists. Dogs suffering from separation anxiety are overly attached (hyperattached) to their owners and become anxious when their owners are not within their sight or leave home without them. These animals usually begin to vocalize (bark, yap, whine), destroy objects, and sometimes soil in the house almost immediately after the owner leaves. In some cases, the dogs may try to escape their confinement, drool, pant, pace, vomit, or lick or chew themselves. They may develop diarrhea, become depressed, and refuse to eat.

Separation anxiety should not be confused with destructive behavior or elimination in the home brought on by the animal being bored and confined for a long period of time. Separation anxiety and inappropriate eliminations should also be differentiated from other possible medical problems, such as metabolic or hormonal problems, cognitive dysfunction (senility), urinary tract infections, or colitis.

The following are some tips to help you deal with your Shih Tzu's separation anxiety.

- Develop a predictable daily routine, so your Shih Tzu knows what to expect and when.
- Offer rewards (food treats, interesting toys, praise, games) for good, calm behavior only. For example, ask your dog to sit and reward her. As she calms, she can receive more affection and praise and more rewards. Gradually extend the time period required for your Shih Tzu to relax and calm down before giving the reward. Dogs that suffer from separation anxiety

usually prefer affection and attention to food rewards.
- Ignore undesirable behavior.
- Never give rewards for bad or demanding behavior or when your Shih Tzu seeks to cling to you.
- Set up a special area for your Shih Tzu and give her some chew toys, food rewards, and even an old piece of your clothing (for scent). Leave the area for a short time period and return with a reward for calm, good behavior. Gradually extend the time away before returning with a reward.
- Counter-conditioning can be helpful. For example, if certain departure cues, such as picking up your car keys or putting on your coat, make your Shih Tzu anxious, try doing these actions without leaving and then reward your Shih Tzu for calm, good behavior.
- Make sure that your Shih Tzu has a chance to play, exercise, and eliminate before you leave for any period of time.
- Leave the house when your Shih Tzu is calm, not excited, or when she is asleep or distracted with a toy or activity.
- Do not make a big deal out of your departure, such as lots of worried baby-talk and hugs. Be matter-of-fact and calm about leaving the house.
- When you return, do not act super excited and emotional to see your Shih Tzu. Be calm and simply ask your Shih Tzu to sit or lie down. Then, reward her only when she is calm.

Separation anxiety may take weeks or months to improve. With a combination of behavior modification (and sometimes drug therapy), most cases improve.

shoe. By doing so, you are telling her that *all* shoes are all right to chew. She will not know the difference between an old shoe and a brand new one. You can prevent your Shih Tzu from chewing on the wrong things if you:

- give your Shih Tzu lots of interesting, safe, chew toys;
- supervise your puppy's chewing activities at all times;
- make sure all valuables (furniture, shoes, books) and harmful items (children's toys, bones, pieces of plastic) are out of your puppy's reach;
- prevent boredom and give your Shih Tzu lots of attention and exercise and take her out on frequent walks.

If your Shih Tzu chews on something she should not, do not shout at her. Simply distract her by offering her one of her own chew toys. Do not chase her to take the object away. She might think you are playing a game and this will reinforce her behavior. Do not use any form of physical punishment. This cruel method will not correct the problem and it will make your Shih Tzu fearful and distrusting of you.

Dealing with Play Biting

Puppies and dogs play with their mouths. Dogs may lightly bite each other in play, but your Shih Tzu should learn from the very beginning that biting humans, even playfully, is *never* allowed. Puppies allowed to bite people when they play, grow up into dogs that think it is all right to bite. Just like adult teeth, puppy teeth are sharp weapons that can injure and inflict pain, especially to children.

If your Shih Tzu bites when you are playing, say "Ouch!" and then "No!" Immediately give your Shih Tzu a chew toy to redirect her actions and modify her behavior. She will quickly learn that chew toys are all right to chew, but biting fingers and hands is not allowed. If your Shih Tzu continues to bite, proceed to the next level. After you say "Ouch" and "No," give her a "time out" and ignore your puppy for ten minutes. Shih Tzu hate to be ignored, so you will probably only have to do this a few times before your puppy learns her lesson.

Never hit, swat, strike, shake, or physically punish your puppy.

Breed Needs

Dominance-based training, such as harsh, loud words or choke collars, is completely inappropriate for Shih Tzu. These techniques will not resolve Shih Tzu behavior problems and will definitely make them much worse. By using physical punishment when a Shih Tzu misbehaves, the trainer is simply temporarily suppressing the behavior. The trainer is not identifying and removing the cause of the behavior, nor is the trainer changing the dog's behavior. Dominance-based training can cause a Shih Tzu to be more fearful of people and things in general and to distrust her owner.

CAUTION

The Three-Second Rule

Owners should try to stop or change their dog's unwanted behavior within three seconds of when it takes place. Granted, this can be challenging, but the more immediate the correction, the more effective it will be. A behavior that is not immediately stopped or modified becomes a reinforced behavior, or a habit. If the misbehavior took place a few minutes in the past, do not try to discipline your Shih Tzu about it. She will not make the association between your displeasure and something she did several minutes, or hours ago.

Dealing with Fear-Related Aggression

Shih Tzu are not naturally aggressive dogs. In fact, they are just the opposite. They were bred to be trusting and friendly. Aggression is a very serious character flaw in a Shih Tzu. Often, fear-related behavior can be mistaken for aggression. For example, if a Shih Tzu barks or growls or lunges at a person or animal, it may be because the dog is frightened and not because it is aggressive. If the behavior is fear-related, the only way to resolve the problem is to identify and address the underlying fear.

Never use physical punishment, or dominance-based training, to treat fear-related aggression. Your Shih Tzu may identify the punishment with the presence of the person or object that initially caused the fear, thereby making the Shih Tzu even more fearful of the person or object in the future.

Breed Truths

Continual destructive chewing is the result of a lack of appropriate environmental enrichment and interesting chew toys, boredom, noise phobias, frustration, confinement anxiety, separation anxiety, or obsessive compulsive disorders.

In addition to destructive chewing, some bored and frustrated Shih Tzu may lick and chew on their feet, legs, and other body parts until they develop sores. This is called self-mutilation.

Communicating with Your Shih Tzu _____

Voice The intonation and volume of your voice tells your Shih Tzu your moods. Your voice tells your dog if you are pleased with her, happy to see her, calm and relaxed, or angry, frightened, or sad. Your words are important, too. Your Shih Tzu has the innate ability to quickly associate certain words and behaviors by listening to you and watching you, so be sure to give each activity a word or phrase and always use the same words or phrases for a given action. For example, if you always say, "Let's ride in the car," when you jingle your car keys, or if you always say, "Go for a walk," when you hold the leash, your Shih Tzu will quickly learn what you mean through a consistent combination of voice, words, and actions.

Hands Hands are one of your greatest tools for communicating with your Shih Tzu. Shih Tzu are sensitive to touch and very attentive to hand movements. From the first time you hold your Shih Tzu, you communicate friendship, affection, and protection to her through gentle, comforting handling. Hands are used to feed meals, bathe, brush, play games, lift, hold, carry, caress, and praise. Hands hold the leash, toys, brush, and food rewards. Hands are powerful tools for communicating and training your Shih Tzu. Take advantage of her interest in your hands to teach hand signal commands early in life. In her senior years, if your Shih Tzu develops hearing difficulty, she can still understand through hand signals (assuming her vision is still good enough to see what you are signaling). Never correct or discipline your Shih Tzu using any form of physical punishment (such as swatting the nose or bridge of the nose, swatting or striking the body, shaking by the scruff of the neck, rolling the animal over onto her back or "alpha rollovers," or squeezing or pushing her to the floor). **Never use your hands to inflict pain or discomfort in any way.** Such cruelty can permanently destroy a Shih Tzu's trust in you and other people, destroy the bond you have formed with your pet, and prevent future communication and understanding for the life of the animal.

Facial Expressions Shih Tzu are people pleasers. They have developed an uncanny ability to read people's facial expressions. Your Shih Tzu relies on a combination of facial expressions, body movements, and voice intonations, to recognize whether you are delighted to see her, pleased with her performance, or unhappy with her behavior.

Body Movement

Body movement is a very important way of communicating with your Shih Tzu and is often tied in closely with hand signals. Shih Tzu are sensitive to rapid, abrupt movements, so always move calmly, smoothly, and gently when you are near your Shih Tzu or when you pick her up and hold her. If you are displeased with your Shih Tzu's behavior, sometimes something as simple as turning away and ignoring her can be a clear message that her behavior is unacceptable. Shih Tzu want to be the center of attention and they hate to be ignored!

Scents

Scent is an important form of communication for all dogs. You can take advantage of your Shih Tzu's keen sense of smell to communicate information to her. For example, your Shih Tzu knows you are going to feed her when she smells the food you prepare for her. In the same way, you can communicate other things to your Shih Tzu through scent. For example, if you are going to leave the house for a short time, use a special scent (for example, a lavender spray) a few minutes before you leave, to condition your Shih Tzu so she learns to associate that particular scent with your temporary absence, just as she might associate a sound, such as the jingle of car keys, to your imminent departure. You can use different scents to communicate a variety of situations to your Shih Tzu. To add to your Shih Tzu's sense of well-being and security, consider giving your Shih Tzu an old shirt you have worn and no longer want that she can call her own and keep in her bed to comfort her when you are away.

Chapter Three

How to Choose a Shih Tzu

The first steps to finding a healthy Shih Tzu are to learn as much as possible about the breed, make sure a Shih Tzu is the right dog for you, and find a reputable Shih Tzu source. A knowledgeable Shih Tzu breeder is the best source for a healthy, well-socialized Shih Tzu. Take time to visit breeders and ask them questions. Finally, use good judgment and choose wisely when you select your Shih Tzu. You are making a long-term commitment. You and your Shih Tzu will be sharing many years together. It must be a perfect match!

Is a Shih Tzu the Best Dog for You?

Every Shih Tzu has its own unique personality and so does every Shih Tzu owner. Shih Tzu also have distinct behavioral and inherited (genetic) traits distinctive of the breed—traits that are deeply engrained in these gentle, good-natured little dogs. The same characteristics that have made the Shih Tzu a treasured pet for centuries are the same ones that make the Shih Tzu a precious companion today: a friendly, outgoing personality, small size, beautiful coat, and an extremely affectionate nature.

Your Shih Tzu will want to be with you every chance she can, so if you are planning to add a Shih Tzu to your life, be sure that a Shih Tzu is the right dog for you!

1. Do you enjoy the company of a dog that is beautiful, elegant, and portable?
2. Are you looking for a dog that is gentle, well-behaved, and affectionate?
3. Do you have lots of time and love to give a little dog that craves attention, loves pampering, and wants to be part of every family activity?
4. Can you afford to feed your dog quality nutrition?
5. Do you have a veterinarian for your Shih Tzu and can you provide her with regular and emergency health care?

6. Do you have time to exercise your Shih Tzu every day?
7. Do you enjoy grooming and do you have the time to do it?
8. Do you have the time and patience to train your companion?
9. Are you prepared to care for a dog for possibly 15 years or more?
10. Have you learned as much as you can about the Shih Tzu breed, and compared it to other breeds, and still believe a Shih Tzu is the best match for you?

If you have answered "yes" to these questions, then you just might be ready to join the ranks of thousands of people who have owned and loved Shih Tzu!

Shih Tzu Choices

One of the best things about Shih Tzu is that no two are alike. Every Shih Tzu is a unique individual, differing from all the others in character, color, markings, personality, and potential. This is what makes choosing a Shih Tzu so much fun—and also so difficult! Perhaps the hardest part of all is leaving the other Shih Tzu behind once you have chosen your favorite one in the group. Shih Tzu are thieves of hearts. Be careful. You might come home with two Shih Tzu instead of one!

When choosing a Shih Tzu, always remember that the most important considerations are the animal's health, personality, and temperament. Age, sex, color, and markings are secondary.

Puppy, Adolescent, or Adult?

Do you want a puppy, an adolescent, or an adult Shih Tzu? It can be a tough decision. Shih Tzu puppies are irresistibly cute, but they are puppies for only a few short months. During that time they require constant care, attention, patience, and

dedication. Shih Tzu puppies can be challenging to raise and train. For some people, a well-mannered adolescent or adult Shih Tzu is a better choice.

Sometimes breeders have adolescent or young adult dogs available for new homes. These dogs may be animals that were retained for the show ring but did not turn out conformation-wise as the breeder had hoped, or they may be retired breeders, or even retired champions. These Shih Tzu are usually trained and well-mannered, so a new owner can bypass the challenges of puppy-hood and housetraining.

It is wise to give the adoption a trial period to be sure you and your new Shih Tzu are a good match and that she will successfully adapt to a change of lifestyle.

Shih Tzu breeders invest a lot of time, effort, training, and money in their animals. The older an animal is, the greater the investment. Most adult Shih Tzu are more expensive than puppies.

The price you pay for your Shih Tzu is insignificant compared to what your pet will cost in training, feeding, grooming, supplies, toys, housing, and veterinary care during the animal's long lifetime. Make sure you have time for a Shih Tzu and can afford one, not just now, but also in the years to come.

Breed Truths

Shih Tzu puppies are tiny and need time to develop and grow. They should not leave the breeder's home before 8 weeks of age. Ideally, they should not be placed in a new home until they are at least 10 to 12 weeks old. **Note:** It is against the law in many states to sell a puppy before it is 8 weeks old.

Personality

Everything a Shih Tzu experiences in her life can affect her personality and behavior. The most critical and formative stage of Shih Tzu behavioral development is from 3 to 12 weeks of age. A Shih Tzu's personality is already well established by the time she is 8 to 12 weeks old. Bonding, socialization, and handling during a Shih Tzu's formative stage are extremely important. Frequent handling in a kind and gentle manner from birth; exposure to various sights and sounds in a nonfrightening and reassuring way; meeting new people and animals; exploring new places; and investigating new and interesting toys, are all part of the socialization process. A well-socialized Shih Tzu is confident, happy, outgoing, friendly, and very trusting. She is also much easier to train than a Shih Tzu that has not had the benefit of numerous positive experiences.

Fun Facts

All Shih Tzu in existence today are the descendents of fourteen dogs: seven males and seven females. Not every one of the fourteen dogs that are the foundation of the Shih Tzu breed were Shih Tzu. One of them was a Pekingese!

Male or Female?

Shih Tzu are wonderful, devoted, loving companions. Whether you decide on a male or a female, the choice is simply a matter of personal preference. Some people claim that male Shih Tzu are more affectionate, calm, even tempered, and willing to please than females. Perhaps that is because some female Shih Tzu act like little divas at times. They can be demanding of your attention and affection and a bit bossy with other dogs, especially if they are jealous of them. The truth is that every Shih Tzu is different. Although there are certain characteristics and behaviors set in the breed, every Shih Tzu is an individual with a unique personality. Each Shih Tzu's traits and temperament are influenced by numerous factors. Socialization, past experiences, genetics, environment, *and the owner* all play a role in the formation of a Shih Tzu's character. In addition, Shih Tzu that are not neutered may have behavioral changes influenced by hormonal fluctuations.

Companion or Show Shih Tzu?

All Shih Tzu are, first and foremost, companions. They were bred specifically for that very purpose, to bond closely with their owners and to provide constant companionship. So when a breeder asks you if you are looking for a companion or a show dog, the question might seem odd at first. What the breeder really wants to know is: Do you plan to participate and seriously compete in dog shows with your Shih Tzu? The breeder will also want to know if you have any intentions of breeding your Shih Tzu or raising them.

All Shih Tzu are companions, but not all Shih Tzu are show dogs. A companion Shih Tzu is an attractive, entertaining, loving member of the family. Shih Tzu destined for the show ring are also very devoted companions.

They must also closely adhere to certain breed standards and expectations regarding height, conformation, character, and gait. A companion Shih Tzu may have minor imperfections when compared to the high conformation standards of a future champion, but be wonderful in all other aspects. The differences between a show Shih Tzu and a companion Shih Tzu are obvious to the trained eye of a breeder, judge, or other dog experts, but may not be readily apparent to the general public.

If you have decided that you want a show dog, be prepared to pay more for it than you would pay for a companion pet. Also, keep in mind that although the parents may be champions, there is no guarantee their puppy will turn out to be a champion, too. If you buy a puppy, you are gambling that it will grow up to be a show winner. If you buy an adult dog, there is no guessing as to how the animal will mature. The developmental stages are completed and what you see is what you get. You can then continue to improve your Shih Tzu's health, coat quality, appearance, and attitude with good nutrition, care, grooming, exercise, and training.

Helpful Hints

Show Dog or Show Off?

Just because the puppies' parents are champions doesn't mean the puppies will also be champions! No one can predict with certainty that a puppy will become a champion, although experienced breeders can detect puppies with potential. Puppies constantly change as they develop and grow. The true test of a show prospect is her ability to win among the top competitors in the show ring.

Coats of Many Colors

Shih Tzu come in many coat colors and patterns and all are permissible and considered equally acceptable for the show ring (see Chapter 1, "All About Shih Tzu," page 11). The only rule in the breed standard is that noses, lips and eyelid margins must be black and eyes should be dark. There are some exceptions to the rules. For example, a liver- or blue-colored Shih Tzu's pigmentation must complement its coat color. Blue eyes do occur in Shih Tzu (one or both eyes); however, the standard requires both eyes to be dark. **Note:** Blue eyes are not visually defective. Just like people, Shih Tzu with blue eyes can see just as well as Shih Tzu with brown eyes.

Age and Longevity

Toy breeds live longer than larger breeds, and the Shih Tzu is a good example. With loving care and good nutrition, Shih Tzu can live up to

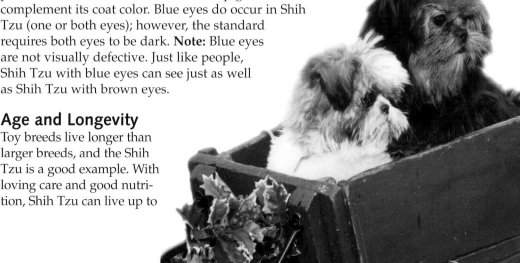

18 years. When you bring a Shih Tzu into your life you are making a long-term commitment. Take your time and choose your new companion very carefully. You will be spending many, many years together!

Finding a Breeder

Breeding and raising quality Shih Tzu is hard work. It is also a very expensive endeavor that is time-consuming, demanding, and challenging. Successful Shih Tzu breeders have years of experience and a solid understanding of the breed, its characteristics, special needs, and genetics.

The best source for a reputable Shih Tzu breeder is the American Shih Tzu Club's Web site (*www.shihtzu.org*). This Web site gives links to Shih Tzu clubs throughout the United States, breeder referrals, and rescue groups.

Another way to find reputable Shih Tzu breeders is to attend dog shows and join a dog club. It is a perfect way to meet other Shih Tzu enthusiasts, including breeders, owners, trainers, handlers, and groomers who can help you find a dedicated breeder who sells healthy, quality Shih Tzu.

CAUTION

Beware of sellers who advertise puppies on the Internet from photographs and who do not thoroughly interview you, or who try to pressure you into a sale, or who are more interested in receiving your payment than they are in the type of home you can provide their dogs. These are not dedicated breeders and some are Internet scams.

Not all breeders are equally dedicated to the breed and its health. Shih Tzu are so much in demand that many people, eager to profit from this toy breed's enormous popularity, raise and sell Shih Tzu in large numbers, with money foremost in mind and with little regard for the animals' health and welfare. Be wary of these individuals.

Reputable Shih Tzu breeders invest the necessary amount of time and money to provide their animals the love, care, training, grooming, housing, exercise, nutrition, and veterinary care they need. These Shih Tzu breeders seldom profit from dog sales because their investment is so great. Theirs is a labor of love. They raise Shih Tzu to improve the breed's beauty, health, and genetics. They do not cut corners when it comes to their dogs' care. They give their Shih Tzu the very best and it shows.

Dog magazines, available at local bookstores and pet stores, are filled with advertisements offering Shih Tzu for sale. One of the many disadvantages of buying a dog from a magazine advertisement is that it may not be possible to make an appointment to meet the breeder and visit the puppies in person. It is important to call the breeder directly, ask questions, and check references before making a purchase.

Newspapers are definitely *not* a good source for finding a Shih Tzu. Reputable breeders have a waiting list for their puppies and do not advertise in newspapers. Many puppies for sale in newspapers are not purebred Shih Tzu, but mixed breeds that are the product of backyard breeding by amateurs, without regard to health, quality, or genetics. To the untrained eye some of these animals may resemble a Shih Tzu, but their personalities and dispositions will be very different. Quality Shih Tzu are good-natured, affectionate, and trusting. Many mixed breeds that are falsely advertised as Shih Tzu often have aggressive or undesirable behaviors. Beware of these sellers and their animals.

Buyer Beware

There is a black market for Shih Tzu. Many Shih Tzu are stolen and sold out of state or used for breeding, usually in puppy mills (also known as puppy factories and puppy

Breed Truths

There is no such thing as a "teacup," "miniature," "imperial," "munchkin," or "dwarf" Shih Tzu. These are runt puppies that are much smaller than normal for their age and usually remain stunted, even as adults. Shih Tzu adults that weigh less than the nine pound minimum required by the breed standard are often the product of bad genetics combined with poor breeding practices. These undersized animals result from extreme inbreeding, malnutrition, heavy parasitism, genetic disorders, and other health problems. Unethical breeders often try to sell undersized Shih Tzu to unsuspecting or uninformed buyers for high prices. These unscrupulous breeders tout their animals to be a "special" variation of the Shih Tzu breed, such as a "teacup," "miniature," "dwarf," or any other cutesy or exotic name they can come up with to misrepresent what they really have—runts that often have serious health problems that usually last throughout their lives. Don't be fooled!

BE PREPARED! Ten Questions to Ask the Breeder

1. How old are the pups and what colors, sexes, and ages are available?

2. Are the pups registered with a recognized kennel club, such as the American Kennel Club?

3. Have the pups been examined and vaccinated by a veterinarian? If so, which vaccinations have the pups received? Do the pups have any special health certifications from veterinary specialists?

4. How many pups are in the litter and at what age were they weaned?

5. Have the pups been treated or tested for internal and external parasites?

6. Does the breeder keep track of and test for health problems? Are there any known health problems in the puppy's family lines?

7. Have the pups received any basic training, including housetraining, crate training, or leash training?

8. What kind of food do the pups eat? How much and how often do they eat?

9. Can you see the parents and littermates of the pup and the environment where the puppies are raised?

10. Will the breeder take the dog back if at some time you are unable to care for her?

farms). Puppy mills breed dogs in large quantities for mass marketing, without regard for the animal's well-being, genetics, quality, or health problems. Puppies are raised in cramped, dirty facilities, with inadequate nutrition, and little human contact. They often have health and behavior problems.

Do not buy your Shih Tzu at a swap meet or in a shopping center parking lot. Huge numbers of toy breeds are illegally smuggled into the United States from Mexico every year. These puppies are taken away from their mothers too early in life, inhumanely transported, tucked away in wheel wells or other dangerous, hidden areas of vehicles without ventilation. These puppies are invariably sick, heavily parasitized, and afflicted with a variety of health and genetic problems.

Do not buy your Shih Tzu from a pet store. Many pet stores procure the puppies they sell from puppy farms. If you buy from a pet store you risk paying a high price for a very poor quality animal. Reputable Shih Tzu breeders never sell their puppies to pet stores. As you interview breeders, be sure to ask the following list of questions:

- How long has the breeder been raising and showing Shih Tzu?
- Is the breeder a member of the American Shih Tzu Club (ASTC)?
- Is the breeder highly recommended by the ASTC?
- Does the breeder belong to local or state dog clubs?
- Does the breeder offer a health and genetics guarantee?

- Does the breeder have a sales contract?
- Does the breeder require a spay/neuter agreement?
- Does the breeder have registration papers, pedigrees, and health certifications available to review?
- Does the breeder provide a 48- to 72-hour health guarantee to give you time to have the puppy examined and declared healthy by your veterinarian?
- Will the breeder take the dog back, at any time during her life, if something happens and you are no longer able to take care of her?

Dedicated Breeders

When you find a reputable Shih Tzu breeder, be prepared to wait for the right puppy or dog. Do not be surprised if the breeder does not have a Shih Tzu immediately available for you. Top breeders have a waiting list for their dogs. Shih Tzu are very popular and in great demand, they take time to mature, and they do not produce large litters. If you have special preferences as to the conformation, sex, age, or color of the Shih Tzu you desire, then it may take longer to find a little "lion dog" that fits your specifications. Keep in mind that your Shih Tzu's health, temperament, and personality are more important than its sex, color, or markings.

You will have a lot of questions for breeders as you search for your perfect pet. The breeders will have plenty of questions for you, too. Their top priority is placing their dogs in an ideal home environment. Shih Tzu can live up to 15 years or more and they require a lot of care and attention. Owning a Shih Tzu is a huge commitment. Breeders do their best to make sure they select the right owners for their animals. When Shih Tzu breeders ask you a lot of questions, it might seem more like an interrogation than an interview, but it shows that they are truly concerned about their animals' well-being. It is up to you to convince the breeder that you are prepared and able to accept the long-term care commitment a Shih Tzu requires—and that you are delighted to do so.

Choosing a Shih Tzu Puppy

You have decided a Shih Tzu is the right dog for you and you have found some reputable Shih Tzu sources. Now comes the fun part—and the most difficult part: choosing a Shih Tzu that is the perfect match for you and your lifestyle. Shih Tzu have long lifespans, you and your dog will be together for many years, so *take your time and use good judgment* as you search for your ideal canine companion.

Whenever possible, once you have located a breeder, call and ask for an appointment to meet the breeder and to see the available puppies, and the puppies' parents, in person. Before the visit, ask the breeder for references. The breeder will also ask you for references, including your veterinarian's name and phone number.

Ask the breeder if the puppies have been registered with an official kennel club, such as the American Kennel Club and if they or their parents have any additional certifications or testing to indicate freedom of inherited health problems known to occur more frequently in the breed (see "Shih Tzu Health and Nutrition" page 77 and also "Special Considerations" page 145).

When you arrive at the breeder's, take note of the animals' home environment, including cleanliness, odors, housing, and play areas. Observe the

BE PREPARED! A Dozen Questions the Breeder Will Ask You

1. Why do you want a Shih Tzu? What do you want or expect from your Shih Tzu? What are your plans for her?

2. Do you have experience with Shih Tzu, or have you owned a Shih Tzu in the past?

3. Do you have the necessary time and money to properly care for a Shih Tzu now and in the long-range future?

4. What kind of home can you provide? (Note: Shih Tzu should be housed indoors only!)

5. Do you have other pets or children in the home? If so, what type of pets and how old are the children?

6. Do you enjoy grooming and do you have time and patience to learn how to do it right? Can you afford to hire a groomer on a frequent, regular basis?

7. Do you have a fenced-in yard, patio, or safe enclosure for a Shih Tzu?

8. How many hours a day are you home? Do you have time to care for your Shih Tzu, including playtime and daily walks?

9. Can you provide the name and phone number of your veterinarian for a reference and follow-up contact?

10. Can the breeder meet all members of your family who will be living with the Shih Tzu?

11. Do you plan to take your Shih Tzu with you on trips and vacations? If not, who will care for your Shih Tzu while you are away?

12. Do you promise to contact the breeder immediately in the event that you are no longer able to keep or care for your Shih Tzu?

puppies closely. Are they healthy, happy, alert, active, and playful? A Shih Tzu is bright, confident, outgoing, trusting, and inquisitive. After a gentle, friendly, introduction, your Shih Tzu should be interested in you and want to cuddle or play. Hiding, trembling, growling, or nipping in fear are completely unacceptable Shih Tzu behaviors. Any puppy that responds to you in this manner should be immediately eliminated from your candidate list.

While you are holding your favorite Shih Tzu puppy, check the eyes, ears, nose, mouth, gums, teeth, skin, and coat. The eyes should be clear and bright. The ears should be clean and free of discharge and bad odor. Normal gums are bright pink in

CHECKLIST

Is the Puppy Healthy?

✔ Overall impression: Healthy, clean, alert, active, attractive very good body condition, attractive fluffy coat, normal gait and movement

✔ Eyes: Bright, clear, free of discharge

✔ Ears: Clean, free of dirt, discharge, and wax buildup; no bad odor; no head-shaking; no scratching at the ears

✔ Nose: Clean, no signs of discharge, nostrils unobstructed and not pinched closed

✔ Mouth: Gums pink, teeth correctly aligned or slightly undershot, when adult teeth are erupting the gums may be temporarily swollen and sore, no duplicate teeth (deciduous and adult of the same type)

✔ Skin and coat: Healthy skin; thick, well-groomed coat free of knots, mats, sores, and parasites

✔ Body condition: Body a little plump, not thin; should not have a grossly distended belly

✔ Movement: Normal gait for a puppy, bouncy and prancing and sometimes a little clumsy

color. Make sure all the teeth are present. If some of the adult teeth are coming in, the baby (deciduous) teeth should have fallen out where the adult teeth are erupting. If the baby teeth do not come out when the adult teeth grow in, there are too many teeth in the mouth and dental problems result. Retained deciduous teeth must be extracted. Teeth should be in correct alignment and all present; however, a missing tooth is not uncommon in Shih Tzu and is not considered a serious fault in the breed.

Shih Tzu can have a slightly undershot bite (the lower jaw protrudes outward past the upper jaw), although ideally jaws should align. The lips should also align properly. If the upper jaw protrudes over the bottom jaw, this is considered a fault. The teeth and tongue should not be visible when the mouth is closed.

Check the skin to be sure it is free of parasites, flakiness, lumps, bumps, or sores. A Shih Tzu puppy's coat is thick and fluffy. It should be well groomed and free of knots and mats. Look under the tail to be sure the area is clean and there are no signs of blood or diarrhea.

Ask to see your pick puppy's litter-mates and parents. The mother is usually

Helpful Hints

Some dogs labeled as "Shih Tzu" that are available for adoption in animal shelters are not really pure Shih Tzu but are mixed breeds that may be part Shih Tzu, or simply resemble a Shih Tzu. These dogs may be aggressive, or have unpredictable and undesirable behaviors that are not typical of a Shih Tzu's trusting, affectionate disposition. Do not confuse mixed breeds with a true Shih Tzu.

available to see, but the father may belong to another breeder and may live far away, out of state, or even out of the country.

When you observe the personalities, behaviors, and appearances of the parents and the littermates, you have a better idea of how your chosen Shih Tzu might look and behave as an adult. Of course, the way you raise and handle your Shih Tzu puppy, and her various experiences, have a big influence on her character development.

Plan to spend lots of time with your Shih Tzu. The more time you spend cuddling, socializing, and training your puppy, the more confident, well-behaved, and happy she will be as an adult.

Kennel Club Registration

When you purchase your Shih Tzu, make sure that she has been registered with a *recognized* kennel club, such as the American Kennel Club (AKC). The registration is proof that your dog is a purebred, genuine Shih Tzu. The registration is also an open door to the pleasures of competing in many official dog activities. Without registration papers, there is no proof of your dog's parentage or breed and your dog cannot participate in many kennel club events.

CAUTION

Don't Be an Impulse Buyer!

It is easy to fall under the charm of the first Shih Tzu you find, but that captivating creature may not be the best match for you. Take time to visit as many breeders and look at as many puppies as possible before you make your final choice. The Shih Tzu you select should be healthy, outgoing, well socialized, and well bred. Do not buy a Shih Tzu puppy that is reclusive, fearful, or overly shy. Do not buy a Shih Tzu puppy that is seriously undersized (runt), weak, or shows even the slightest signs of illness. It is normal to feel sorry for these animals, but don't let sympathy distract your focus from an affectionate, confident, healthy puppy. Shy, sick puppies can mean serious medical or behavioral problems now and in the future, as well as significant medical expenses and possible heartbreak later. Use your head: Consider only the most healthy, friendly, confident, outgoing puppies. Then use your heart for your final selection among them.

Reputable breeders register their litters. Be wary of any breeder who cannot provide you with proof of litter registration. *Official registration is not the same as a pedigree.* Only the kennel club can issue a registration. Anyone can write up a pedigree.

Registration Application When you purchase your Shih Tzu, the breeder will give you a registration application or, if the dog has already been named and registered, the breeder will sign the registration form indicating ownership has been transferred to you. The registration application lists the breeder, the litter registration number, the litter birth date, and the names and registration numbers of your puppy's parents. Whoever registers the dog has the right to name it; however, many breeders request that their kennel name to be included as part of the dog's full registered name.

If you are submitting the registration application form, choose a name for your Shih Tzu and submit the application form to the kennel club address

indicated on the form along with the required registration fee. The American Kennel Club allows you to register online (*www.akc.org*). You will then receive a certificate of registration from the kennel club, with your dog's official name and indicating you as the new owner.

If your Shih Tzu is born in the United States, the breeder will decide whether she receives a full registration or a limited registration.

Full Registration A full registration is printed on a white piece of paper with a purple border. It lists the breeder, the owner, the registered name and number of the dog, its birth date, breed, color, and sex. The dog's parents and their titles or certifications are also indicated. Full registration allows for participation in AKC competitions and events, as well as the ability to register future offspring of the animal with the AKC.

Limited Registration A limited registration contains the same information as a full registration certificate and looks the same except the border is orange. Dogs with limited registration cannot be used for breeding purposes. If they produce puppies, their puppies cannot be registered with the AKC. Only the breeder, not the owner, can change an animal's status from limited to full registration.

Pedigree

A pedigree is a chart showing the dog's family tree. A three-, four-, or five-generation pedigree fits on one page. Breeders often prepare pedigrees for buyers, listing the puppy's parents, grandparents, and

Fun Facts

People who buy dogs without registration papers often wonder later if they really have a purebred after all, or if their dog is a mixed breed. DNA tests can prove an animal's species, and prove that a dog is a dog, but to date there are no available DNA tests to prove a dog is a specific breed. However, there is now a DNA test available to determine which breeds are the ancestors a of mixed breed dog. **Note:** More than 50 percent of dogs in the United States are mixed breeds.

CHECKLIST

What Your Shih Tzu Needs

Before making a final decision, be sure the puppy's health records, kennel club registration papers, and other documents are in order.

✔ Health guarantee from the breeder, including other contractual information such as spay/neuter agreements and return and refund policies

✔ Health certificate signed by a veterinarian stating that the puppy was examined within the past ten days and is healthy

✔ Medical record listing all vaccines and treatments (such as parasite control) the animal has received and the dates they were given, also neuter certificate and date of other medical or surgical procedures, if applicable

✔ Microchip identification number and documentation, including forms for the new owner to register with the microchip data base

✔ Kennel club registration application form or transfer of ownership, signed by the breeder, owner, and co-owner when indicated

✔ Pedigree listing the names, titles, health certifications, and other information about the dog's parents, grandparents, and great-grandparents

✔ Additional documents, such as eye certifications or DNA test results

✔ Dog license and proof of rabies vaccination when applicable

✔ Written care instructions from the breeder, including feeding instructions and recommended diet, veterinarian, grooming parlor, obedience class, dog club

✔ Receipt for purchase of your puppy, indicating date of sale and purchase price

great-grandparents. If you have a pedigree from the breeder, remember that this is not an official document and it does not guarantee that the dog is purebred or registered with a recognized kennel club. However, if you do not have a pedigree, and your Shih Tzu is registered with the AKC, you can order a detailed pedigree, suitable for framing, directly from the AKC. The AKC pedigree lists the names, registration numbers, coat colors, and certain awards and certifications of your Shih Tzu's immediate ancestors.

Shih Tzu Rescue

It is hard to imagine that any Shih Tzu could end up homeless, neglected, or unwanted. Ironically, this breed's extreme popularity is one of the reasons for its high numbers of abandonment and relinquishment at animal shelters.

It often starts with puppy mills that raise Shih Tzu in large numbers, strictly for profit, without regard for health or quality. Impulse buyers add to the problem. They fall in love with a Shih Tzu on the spur of the moment

45

COMPATIBILITY Is a Shih Tzu the Best Breed for You?

ENERGY LEVEL	● ● ●
PERSONAL ATTENTION TIME REQUIREMENT	● ● ● ● ●
EXERCISE REQUIREMENT	● ● ●
PLAYFULNESS	● ● ● ●
AFFECTION LEVEL	● ● ● ● ●
FRIENDLINESS TOWARD OTHER PETS	● ● ● ●
FRIENDLINESS TOWARD STRANGERS	● ● ● ● ●
FRIENDLINESS TOWARD CHILDREN	● ● ● ●
EASE OF TRAINING	● ● ●
GROOMING REQUIREMENTS	● ● ● ● ●
SPACE REQUIREMENTS	● ● ●
OK FOR BEGINNERS	●

5 Dots = Highest rating on scale

OVERVIEW: Shih Tzu training requires lots of patience and skill, together with soft handling and a good understanding of the dog's tolerance level. If incorrectly managed or forced, a Shih Tzu may become willful. Shih Tzu need exercise and quality nutrition. They require extensive, frequent grooming. Shih Tzu demand almost constant attention. They are most suitable for people who have lots of time and patience, who are home most of the day, who enjoy grooming, and who love constant canine companionship.

and buy it without first doing their homework. Too late, they learn that they cannot afford the time or money to give a Shih Tzu the special care it needs.

Some people buy Shih Tzu because they think Shih Tzu ownership is a fashion statement, status symbol, or a sign of wealth. They love to show off their flashy dogs, but eventually lose interest when the next trendy breed comes along.

There are countless reasons that so many adult Shih Tzu are homeless. Reasons include moving; not enough time, space, or money; personal issues (divorce, changing jobs, new baby, illness); or the Shih Tzu is ill and the owner cannot afford veterinary care. Shih Tzu that are not properly socialized as puppies or trained as youngsters, often develop behavior problems and are abandoned at animal shelters. Whatever the reason for relinquishment, the result is tragic. The little toy Shih Tzu, bred to thrive on close human companionship, no longer has a family or home and, if not rescued, will be euthanized. Many rescue Shih Tzu are well-behaved and house-trained. Others may have behavior problems, especially if they have been left alone or ignored for too long, or did not receive enough socialization or training.

BE PREPARED! What Will My Dog Cost Me?

The American Veterinary Medical Association states that the average pet owner spends about $350 annually on veterinary care for each dog owned. The truth is, owning a Shih Tzu could cost from several hundred to several thousand dollars a year. If you are planning on owning a Shih Tzu, be realistic about the financial implications. The following is a guideline of the minimum amount Shih Tzu owner-ship costs per year:

- **Food:** Shih Tzu do not eat much but they require top quality nutrition.Dog food prices vary according to region and quality, and prices continue to rise. Prescription diets are more expensive. $350 to $600
- **Veterinary Care:** Depends on the age, health, and lifestyle of the dog. Veterinary fees vary; specialists' fees are higher. Laboratory tests, surgery, dental work, or a medical emergency can cost hundreds to thousands of dollars. Estimate is for a healthy dog requiring only an annual examination, routine laboratory tests, and vaccinations. $500
- **Accessories:** The basics (crate, exercise pen, collar, leash, bed, dishes, toys, grooming supplies). $350
- **Boarding facility or pet sitter:** $20 to $35 daily
- **Travel:** Additional fee for hotels that accept dogs. $15 to $25 per day plus deposit
- **Liability insurance:** Varies according to insurance company. $50
- **Health insurance:** varies according to insurance company. **Note:** The American Kennel Club offers a health insurance program. $100
- **License:** Varies according to county and state, licenses for neutered dogs are discounted. $15 to $35 per year

If you are up to the challenge of rescuing a Shih Tzu, the experience can be highly rewarding. Contact the American Shih Tzu Club (*www.shihtzu.org*) and the United States Shih Tzu Rescue (*www.usshihtzurescue.com*). Many Shih Tzu, especially older ones, have health problems or special needs. They can be expensive to care for, but they will shower you with love and friendship that money cannot buy.

If you cannot rescue a Shih Tzu at this time, there are lots of other ways you can help these unfortunate animals find loving homes, including donating and volunteering. The rescue organizations will be grateful for your help and so will the Shih Tzu!

Chapter Four

Caring for a Shih Tzu Puppy

Y ou have found your perfect Shih Tzu puppy. Now it is time to bring her home and make her feel safe and comfortable in her new surroundings. Your puppy will adapt quickly to her new family and lifestyle if you have everything prepared and ready *before* you bring her home.

Puppy-Proofing

Some of the characteristics you admire most about your new puppy—her natural inquisitiveness, outgoing personality, small size, and busy activity level—also create some of the biggest problems for her safety.

Before you bring your Shih Tzu home, you must "puppy proof" your house, garage, yard, and garden. Be sure to check *everywhere* for hazards that are potentially dangerous for your puppy. Remove them or block her access to them.

Be careful not to step on your Shih Tzu! Your puppy will try to stick close to you and follow you. She will always be underfoot, so pay attention to where you step.

Closely supervise your Shih Tzu's activities at all times.

The following is a list of what to look out for when puppy-proofing your home.

Scout the area: Get down to puppy eye-level to see what kinds of trouble your Shih Tzu could encounter.

Doors, windows, furniture: Make sure all doors are securely closed. Prevent your Shih Tzu from climbing up on furniture. She could fall and be injured. If the furniture is pushed under an open window, she could fall out the window. She could also get crushed or injured under rocking, gliding, and reclining chairs.

Cabinets: Securely fasten cabinets containing household cleaning products and chemicals. Make sure nothing can fall off shelves onto your puppy.

Baseboards and walls: Check to be sure baseboards and walls have not been painted with toxic paints, such as lead-based paints or toxic varnishes.

Electrical cords and appliances: Unplug electrical cords and move them out of your puppy's reach. Electrocution from gnawing on an electrical cord can kill your Shih Tzu and cause an electrical fire in your home.

Kitchen: Put up a barrier to prevent your puppy from gaining access to the kitchen while you are cooking, so she is not stepped on, burned, or injured.

Toilets: Keep lids down on toilets so your pet cannot drink out of them or climb and fall into them.

Breed Truths

Most cases of Shih Tzu broken bones or injuries are caused by owners accidentally stepping on them, children dropping them, or large dogs attacking them or playing too roughly with them.

Equipment: Many types of common equipment can be dangerous for puppies and cause freak accidents. Accidents happen! Make sure all equipment is turned off and unplugged when your puppy is in the area.

Garage: Place everything—sharp objects, tools, poisons, chemicals, insecticides—out of reach. Antifreeze (ethylene glycol) is a common cause of animal poisoning that can be found on garage floors. It has a sweet taste that attracts animals. Even ingesting a very small amount can cause severe kidney damage and death.

Yard hazards: Check for holes in and under the fence, gates that do not close securely, toxic chemicals, including fertilizers, weed killer, and poison mulch (such as cocoa mulch).

Poisonous plants: Check for poisonous plants in the house and garden, such as philodendron, foxglove, and Lily of the Valley. Keep household plants out of reach and limit home and garden plants to nontoxic varieties. Check with your local nursery about which plants, mulch, and chemicals in your yard may be poisonous.

Foreign objects: Make sure small balls, children's toys, rubber bands, paper clips, pens, sewing needles, string, buttons, coins, and similar small objects are out of your pet's reach. Pennies contain high levels of zinc and can cause zinc poisoning as well as choking.

Garbage: Keep trash out of the reach of your Shih Tzu to prevent her from eating spoiled food, bones, plastic, aluminum, or other dangerous items. "Garbage poisoning" is a common form of food poisoning in dogs. It is caused by bacteria and bacterial toxins found in old and decaying foods.

Candies and medicines: Make sure there are no foods, candies, or medicines within your puppy's reach. Chocolate is toxic for dogs. Hard candies can cause choking and suffocation. An overdose of common medicines, including aspirin, acetaminophen, ibuprofen, and naproxen can be fatal for your Shih Tzu.

Swimming pools and Jacuzzis: Keep pools and Jacuzzis covered; make sure there are no openings in the fence around them.

CAUTION

Grapes of Wrath and Other Foods Toxic to Dogs

Grapes and raisins are toxic for dogs. Just a few grapes or raisins can cause severe kidney damage and death. Chocolate is also responsible for many dog deaths.

Chocolate contains a methylxanthine substance called theobromine that is highly toxic to dogs. Theobromine is also found in cocoa mulch, a popular garden mulch that smells like chocolate. Several canine deaths have been caused by the ingestion of cocoa mulch.

The artificial sweetener, xylitol, found in sugar-free candies and gum, is toxic to dogs. Xylitol causes a sudden drop in the animal's blood sugar and rapid death.

The First Day

Ideally, the breeder will have already introduced your Shih Tzu puppy to a crate (travel kennel) as part of her basic preliminary training. Many breeders use crates as portable doghouses and encourage young puppies to eat, sleep, and play in them. If your puppy is unfamiliar with crates, now is the perfect time for her to learn. You will use a crate often for travel, home, and training.

Place your puppy's favorite toy, or a blanket with familiar scents (such as a blanket that your puppy's mother and littermates have been sleeping on), in the crate for the trip home. A familiar item with comforting smells will help your Shih Tzu feel more secure during the trip and the next few days in her new home environment.

CHECKLIST

What Your Shih Tzu Needs

The following are what your Shih Tzu puppy will need when you bring her home.

✔ Collar: Small collar, such as a break-away cat collar. A buckle collar or slip collar may be used for training but only when under direct supervision. Never leave your pet unattended wearing a slip or choke collar. She could accidentally catch on objects and strangle to death. Check the collar often to make sure it is not too tight as your Shih Tzu grows.

✔ Harness: The advantages of a harness over a collar are that it cannot slip off and cannot choke your puppy. Check the harness frequently and adjust the size as your puppy grows.

✔ Identification tag: Be sure to include your telephone number and an alternate contact telephone number in case you cannot be reached.

✔ Leash: A light leash is all that is necessary for a Shih Tzu. A show lead is ideal. Avoid retractable leashes. They can cause injury and are not good training tools.

✔ Dishes: Food and water dishes should be stainless steel or ceramic. Do not use plastic or rubber dishes; they can cause skin allergies around the mouth and chin.

✔ Water bottle: Shih Tzu can learn to drink from a sipper tube. Bottles can be hung from exercise pens or on travel kennel doors. They are convenient because they do not spill and faces do not get wet.

✔ Food: Feed top-quality puppy food. Consult your veterinarian and the puppy's breeder for recommendations. Do not make sudden changes to your puppy's diet.

✔ Bed, pillows, blankets: Bedding material should be made of natural fibers, such as cotton or wool. Some synthetic materials,

and also bedding containing cedar shavings, can cause allergies.

✔ Crate (plastic travel kennel or wire crate with removable floor pan): Ideal for use as a small doghouse, crates are lightweight, non-porous, easy to clean, well-ventilated, and offer privacy. They are excellent tools for house training. The crate should be large enough for your Shih Tzu to sit, stand, and turn around comfortably.

✔ Exercise pen (x-pen): Exercise pens provide a safe enclosure for puppies to play and exercise in while under supervision. These portable folding pens are available in a variety of sizes, with attachments for dishes and water bottles.

✔ Safety gates: Safety gates are useful barriers for closing off a designated area or stairway to prevent escape or injury.

✔ Grooming supplies: Basic grooming supplies include a slicker brush or stiff bristle brush, wide-toothed metal comb, blunt-tipped scissors, nail trimmers, nail file, styptic powder, gentle emollient or puppy shampoo, conditioning rinse, gentle ear-cleaning solution, hair dryer, soft terry cloth towels, and paper towels.

✔ Toys: Give your puppy lots of safe and interesting toys, such as soft stuffed toys, balls, and indestructible chew toys. Do not buy toys with small bells, whistles, buttons, or other items that can be a choking hazard.

✔ House-training pads: Pads are available from pet stores (also called "wee" pads).

✔ Pooper scooper: Scoopers are available from pet stores and comes in various sizes.

✔ First aid kit: See contents for first aid kit, see Chapter Six, "Shih Tzu Health and Nutrition," page 89.

CAUTION

Never Let Your Shih Tzu Loose in the Car

When your puppy travels for the first time, she may cry or whimper. If she whimpers or cries, talk to her soothingly so she knows she is not alone, but keep her in her crate. If you take her out and hold her, she will expect you to hold her every time she travels. No dog should ever be loose in a car. If there is an accident, your Shih Tzu could be injured by an airbag, thrown into a window, or flung from the vehicle. She could cause an accident by distracting the driver and/or getting underfoot.

The trip from the breeder's to your home may be the first time your Shih Tzu has ever traveled in a car. Give your puppy a chance to urinate and defecate before you place her in the crate. Make sure she has not eaten within an hour of the trip, so she will be less likely to become carsick. If your Shih Tzu feels nauseous, she may drool or vomit, so bring plenty of paper or terry cloth towels and a plastic bag for the trip.

Do not withhold food for more than two hours before travel because your small puppy could become hypoglycemic (have low blood sugar) from the excitement and stress of leaving home, traveling, and joining a new family.

Do not give your Shih Tzu puppy a tranquilizer or sedative when you travel. These can be dangerous for puppies (and some adults).

When you arrive home, give your Shih Tzu a small drink of water. Place her in an area that you want her to use for urination and defecation and give her some time to relax, explore, and relieve herself. Then praise her for eliminating in the right spot. Your puppy will be tired from the trip; if she is sleepy, let her rest. If she feels like becoming acquainted, do so calmly and gently. Avoid loud noises and sudden movements. If you have children in the home, teach them immediately to respect the puppy's space and privacy, speak in soft voices, and do not make sudden movements that might frighten her.

Set up an area near the kitchen or living room where your puppy can be safe, warm, and protected and from which you can easily observe her. You can

use baby gates, barriers, and exercise pens to make a secure enclosure. Place the crate inside the enclosed area and place soft bedding in the crate. You can also put a soft bed outside of the crate, so your puppy can have choices. Let your puppy explore and relax for several minutes. If she enters the crate on her own, praise her.

Place a water bowl in the enclosed area and make sure your puppy has fresh, clean water available at all times.

Continue to feed your Shih Tzu the same food that she was eating at the breeder's. A sudden change in diet could upset her digestive system. If you want to change the type of food your puppy is eating, do it gradually, after consulting with your veterinarian.

Feed your Shih Tzu small, frequent meals throughout the day so that her blood sugar does not get too low (hypoglycemia). She may need as many as six meals daily, or you can feed her free choice, if she does not tend to overeat. Measure your puppy's food and water so you know exactly how much she eats and drinks every day.

Every Shih Tzu's personality is unique. As you get to know your puppy better, you will think of a name that suits your little friend perfectly. When you have selected a name, use it often when talking to your Shih Tzu. It won't take her long to know who she is. When your Shih Tzu responds or comes to you when you say her name, praise her enthusiastically.

CAUTION

Remove the door to the crate when you are not crating your puppy. Her feet can get caught and pinched between the crate and the hinged side of the swinging door if it is not removed.

Crate Training

Crate training is a very important part of your Shih Tzu's education. To start, put the crate in a safe place where your Shih Tzu can feel secure and have some privacy. Make sure you can observe your puppy and she can also watch you and the family. Don't put your puppy's crate in an area where she will be or feel isolated. Exposure to various sights, sounds, smells, activities, and people are very important aspects of puppy socialization.

To start crate training, play with your puppy so that she has a chance to exercise and eliminate. Calmly put her in her crate with a special toy and a treat, securely fasten the crate door, and make the house quiet. Leave your puppy in the crate for ten minutes.

Your puppy will probably fall asleep, but if she stays awake and remains quiet, let her out after ten minutes and praise her. Using this method, gradually extend the time a few minutes daily over the next several days.

When your puppy is used to being in a crate for two hours at a time, you can change the crate training time from day to evening. Take advantage of your puppy's crate training to complement her housetraining. At night, place lots of absorbent bedding in the crate and place the crate in your bedroom so you can hear your puppy if she wakes up and needs to eliminate. Your puppy will do her best not to soil her sleeping quarters. When you take her outside during the night, do not play with her. Just wait for her to do her business, praise her, then put her back in her crate for the rest of the night. Be sure to get up as needed during the night and in the early morning hours to let your puppy do her business. Your Shih Tzu is just a baby! Her bladder is tiny and doesn't hold much. In time, she will be able to control her bladder and bowels for up to six hours overnight and you will both be able to sleep better.

Never use the crate as a tool for punishment. Never put your Shih Tzu in the crate when she has misbehaved. Her crate and enclosed area should always be a comforting place where she goes when all is well, not when she is in trouble.

Helpful Hints

If your Shih Tzu barks, cries, or scratches at the door when she is in her crate, ignore the noise. Do not let her out until she has been quiet for at least five minutes. If you do, your puppy will interpret your actions as a reward for barking and scratching!

Housetraining

Housetraining your Shih Tzu can be a challenge, but with patience, diligence, consistency, and persistence, you both will succeed. The important thing is making sure your puppy receives lots of praise when she does the right thing.

Shih Tzu do their best not to soil where they are housed or confined. This is another reason for keeping your puppy in a travel kennel when you have to leave for *very brief* periods. When you return, your Shih Tzu will have waited to urinate or defecate. Take her to her toilet area immediately upon arrival. Place her where you want her to learn to eliminate. When she eliminates, praise her enthusiastically. Offer your puppy a small food reward so she knows you are pleased.

Helpful Hints

Never keep your Shih Tzu confined in a crate for extended periods of time. If you do, her crate will seem more like a prison than a safe haven or comfortable den and she will not want to go in it.

Next, place your Shih Tzu in her designated living area. This area should have easy-to-clean flooring, such as tile or linoleum (not carpeting). Remember that your puppy does not have full control of her bladder or bowels yet. She will need to go outside frequently and certainly will have a few accidents before she is fully trained. As soon as she understands that she should only urinate or defecate in the area you take her to, your Shih Tzu will try her best to wait until she can make it to that spot.

Do not wait for your Shih Tzu to tell you she needs to go. She will not yet know *how* to tell you. Much like a toddler, a puppy doesn't realize she has to go until the very last moment, sometimes just a few seconds before the event. It is up to you to be attentive to signs of impending urination or defecation so you can take her to her elimination spot in time. Signs of impending elimination include sniffing the ground, pacing, circling, whining, crying, and acting anxious. You must act immediately when you see this behavior begin or you will be too late! If your Shih Tzu soils in her confinement, it is an accident, so don't punish her. *Never raise your voice or shout or use physical punishment of any kind.* That is the

FYI: Litter Box Training

Many Shih Tzu can be trained to use a litter box indoors and will continue to use them when they are adults. Litter boxes are very convenient. They allow your Shih Tzu to relieve herself when you are not home.

Make or buy a shallow litter box (1 to 2 inches deep) that is about 12 inches square or larger. Use paper pellet litter, available from pet stores. Some Shih Tzu prefer to use sand. You can purchase sterile or clean sand from a children's toy store (for sandboxes). Put the litter box in an easy-to-find spot in your pet's enclosure. Make sure she can easily climb into the litter box. Give your puppy the right idea by taking a tiny amount of stool from her last elimination and place it in the box. When your puppy acts like she needs to go outside, quickly place her in the box. When she eliminates in the box, praise her enthusiastically and give her a little food reward.

worst thing you can do. Your Shih Tzu will not associate your scolding with her natural body functions, especially if the scolding occurs some time after the act of elimination. Instead, simply clean up the mess and work on positive reinforcement. Praise your puppy profusely when she does the right thing. It's up to you to make housetraining fun and rewarding so your puppy wants to participate and please you.

One of the keys to successful housetraining is to set up a regular schedule. Ideally, a young puppy should be let outside every few hours. Sometimes this still isn't often enough. Of course, there will be times when you simply cannot be available to do this. When you have to be out of the house for long periods of time, keep your puppy restricted to a designated, confined area and cover the floor of the area with housetraining pads ("wee" pads) or newspapers. Shih Tzu puppies tend to wander about as they eliminate, so although your puppy will try to urinate and defecate on the papers, she may miss them sometimes. Be patient. As your puppy develops more bladder and bowel control, she will also learn to stay in one place when she urinates and defecates.

If weather prohibits taking your puppy outside (snow, rain, cold wind, extreme heat), train her to use housetraining pads or newspapers. Wait until the weather is better before you start taking her outside.

When you take your Shih Tzu out to eliminate, stay and wait with her. If you go into the house, she will be distracted, forget why she was let outside, worry, and try to

Helpful Hints

Puppies always need to urinate immediately after waking up from a nap or after eating a meal, so in these instances, take your Shih Tzu directly to her elimination location without waiting for signs. Remember to always praise her enthusiastically for her good performance.

FYI: Coprophagy

Coprophagy is the act of eating feces. It can be the animal's own feces, or the feces of other animals. Many Shih Tzu develop this behavior. The reasons for coprophagy in dogs are not clear. Many theories have been suggested but no specific cause has yet been proven, nor has any one reliable treatment method been identified. The best thing to do is prevent your Shih Tzu from having access to fecal material.

Clean up your dog's feces as soon as she has completed her bowel movement and prevent her access to the cat litter box. If you live on a farm or ranch, remember that if your Shih Tzu ingests fecal material from other animals, she may contract diseases spread in the feces. She also can be susceptible to poisoning if these animals were recently medicated with drugs to which your Shih Tzu is sensitive.

find you. And if you are in the house, you won't know if your puppy did anything outside. You might bring her back inside before she eliminates and then she could have an accident in the house. That would be a setback in her training.

CAUTION

If your Shih Tzu (puppy or adult) is housetrained and starts having accidents in the house, this could be a sign of medical problems such as a bladder infection or intestinal upset. Consult your veterinarian.

It's also important to check on how your puppy urinates and defecates. If she is having trouble, or has diarrhea or worms, you will not notice unless you are present when she eliminates. (If your puppy has a problem, collect a fresh stool specimen to take to your veterinarian for diagnosis.)

Housetraining requires two-way communication. You teach your Shih Tzu that she must eliminate outside, and she must find a way to let you know her desire to go outside. She may never "ask" to go outside by barking or scratching at the door or fetching her leash like the dogs in the movies. But if she hasn't been outside for a long period of time, or just woke up, or just finished eating, or acts anxious or apprehensive, starts whining and circling, squatting, or starts to pant and stare at you, you know what to do.

House Rules

Your Shih Tzu puppy must learn the house rules. Decide right now what you are willing and not willing to allow your puppy to do. For example, if you do not want your Shih Tzu in a certain part of the house, or on the furniture, or sleeping on your bed, do not allow her to do these things when she is a puppy. She will naturally expect to be able to do these things all of her life.

There are a lot of rules for your puppy to learn, so be patient and give her time. Here are some guidelines that will make your pet a more enjoyable family member.

House limits: Teach your Shih Tzu where she can be in the house and yard and which areas are off limits.

Come: Your puppy should come to you when called.

Barking: Your puppy must learn that constant barking or yapping is not permissible.

Chewing: Teach your Shih Tzu to chew only on chew toys.

Begging: Begging is not allowed. Keep your Shih Tzu out of the kitchen and dining area during mealtimes.

Crate: Your Shih Tzu should learn to be calm and quiet in her crate.

Housetraining: Your Shih Tzu should be housetrained to go outside, use papers, or a litter box.

Manners: Jumping and chasing are not allowed in the house.

Household items: Your puppy must not dig in the potted plants or rummage through the trash.

Patience: Your Shih Tzu should sit and wait for permission before she goes outside. Don't allow her to dart out the door or to pull you on a leash. Teach her to wait for meals by sitting politely until you lower the food bowl and give her the signal that she can eat.

"Drop it" or "Give it": Teach your Shih Tzu to release an item in her mouth that you do not want her to have.

Biting: Your Shih Tzu should not bite you.

Socialization

Socialization is absolutely essential for your puppy to be confident, friendly, well mannered, and well adjusted. It is critical that a puppy receive lots of socialization from 3 to 12 weeks of age, including human contact, handling, petting, and interaction. Most puppies' personalities are set by nine weeks of age. If a puppy is ignored or neglected, she will have social difficulties all of her life, many that cannot be resolved or overcome.

CHECKLIST

Keys to Socialization Training

Here are some things to introduce your Shih Tzu to as part of her socialization training.

✔ Different people in a variety of clothing (ask them to pet and praise your puppy)

✔ Children of various sizes and ages

✔ Dogs, puppies, and other animal species (keep your puppy at a safe distance so she is not injured, especially around larger animals)

✔ Different surfaces to walk on, such as wood, tile, carpet, grass, dirt, cement, and sand

✔ Water: hose, sprinklers, pool, beach, bathtub, rain

✔ Household appliances: hair dryer, vacuum cleaner, washing machine, clothes dryer, dishwasher, blender

✔ Unexpected movement: flags, plastic bags, kites, balloons, umbrellas, tarps

✔ Crowds: parades, parties, dog shows, classrooms

✔ Sounds: music, traffic, airports, sirens, lawnmowers, yard blowers, thunder

✔ Equipment: wheelchairs, walkers, strollers, sporting equipment

✔ Bicycles, scooters, and skateboards.

Puppies are often placed in new homes at eight to eleven weeks of age. This age is sometimes called the "fear imprint period" because during this age, anything negative that happens to the animal seems to impact her for life. This is a critical time to focus on building your Shih Tzu's confidence. Make sure all of her experiences are good ones. Never behave as though your Shih Tzu has something to fear. If you baby your Shih Tzu or cuddle her protectively, this will reinforce her fear

PERSONALITY POINTERS

Common Shih Tzu Puppy Behavior Problems

Behavior Problem	What to Do
Barking	Do not reward your puppy by paying attention to her when she barks. Ignore her and wait until she is quiet, or distract her by asking her to sit. When she has stopped barking, give her attention, a toy, or a treat.
Biting	Do not allow your puppy to play bite or chew on your fingers. Say, "Ouch! No!" Stop playing. Wait a short time. When your puppy has calmed down, ask her to sit, or distract her with a toy.
Chewing	Do not allow your puppy to chew on anything except her chew toys. Tell her "Drop it," or "Give it" (use the same words every time) and take the toy from her. Do not pull on it or she will think it is a tug-of-war game. Distract her with a chew toy, and when she takes her chew toy, praise her.
Jumping	Do not pick your puppy up and cuddle her when she jumps. Distract her and change her behavior by telling her to sit. Make sure she sits in place for at least a few seconds, then reward her with praise or a small treat for sitting. Make sure she knows the reward is for sitting calmly, and *not* for jumping.

behavior and make her think there was actually something to fear. Instead, speak to her calmly (or enthusiastically and playfully, depending on the circumstance) and continue to gradually introduce her to different people, places, and things.

Socialization should be a lifelong process. Always praise your Shih Tzu for confident, outgoing, good behavior. Make socialization a fun game—for life.

Introduce your puppy to new people, places, and things—but not all at once! Make all her experiences positive ones and give her lots of praise. Early socialization will make your Shih Tzu more confident, and will help her cope with unexpected, noisy, and frightening events, such as thunderstorms and alarms.

Helpful Hints

Newborn puppies spend 90 percent of their time sleeping and 10 percent eating. For the first four weeks of life, activated sleep (muscle tics, twitching, jerking) is a very important part of puppy sleep. These movements are normal. It is abnormal if a puppy does not twitch during sleep.

Puppy Health and Nutrition

Your Shih Tzu's health care starts from birth. If your puppy's mother and breeder took good care of her, you are both off to a great start. If your puppy's early weeks were rough—for example, if she is a runt or suffered from poor nutrition, an illness, or injury—then she has some catching up to do. Either way, your puppy depends on you to feed her the best food and give her the best care to keep her healthy from the first day you bring her home—and for the rest of her life. Good health care and nutrition today means fewer health problems later on and a longer life for your Shih Tzu.

Exercise is important. Play games with your puppy and take her on little walks. Keep in mind that she is very small and that for every one of your steps, your puppy has to take several. Don't overdo it! She does not have a lot of endurance, so don't overexert or exhaust her. Keep games and activities at a level you both can enjoy. Remember, too, that your puppy is very low to the ground. Do not make her walk on surfaces that can be very hot in summer, such as asphalt, cement, and sand. She could burn her belly as well as her footpads.

Shih Tzu puppies need regular brushing, just like adults. Brushing keeps the skin healthy. You must take care of your puppy's coat from the very beginning, so she is used to grooming and so her coat can grow long and gorgeous. Every time you brush your puppy's coat, check for parasites and skin sores.

Take your puppy to your veterinarian for a health checkup within 72 hours of bringing her home. Use her crate to transport her and bring a blanket with you. After your veterinarian has disinfected the exam tabletop, put your puppy's blanket on the table and set her on it while your veterinarian conducts the physical examination. That way she will not get cold from the stainless steel tabletop and she will not come in contact with germs from other animals that were on the table. Remember to wash the blanket when you return from the veterinarian's. Your puppy is not considered fully protected against some contagious diseases until she has had her third set of vaccinations at 16 weeks of age.

Your veterinarian will check your Shih Tzu for internal and external parasites, listen to her heart and lungs, palpate her lymph nodes and body organs, check her eyes, ears, and mouth, make dietary recommendations, discuss care, recommend a vaccination schedule, and answer your questions.

Shih Tzu puppies have a tendency to accumulate discharge in the corners of their nose and eyes. Be sure to gently wipe the inside corners of your puppy's eyes with a warm, soft, damp, clean cloth, as needed. Clean the nostrils gently using a different cloth, so you do not transfer germs to your puppy's eyes from her nostrils or mouth. If the eye or nasal discharge is excessive or contains pus, contact your veterinarian immediately.

Check inside your puppy's ears and clean them gently with a soft, damp cloth, as needed. Use a separate cloth for each ear. Do not use ear cleaners containing alcohol. They can burn and irritate your Shih Tzu's delicate ears. Allow the ears to dry.

Practice brushing your puppy's teeth with a very soft toothbrush once a week.

This is good training so you can brush her adult teeth later in life. Your Shih Tzu's deciduous (baby) teeth will have all fallen out by the time she is six or seven months old.

Trim the very tips of your puppy's nails at least once a month. It is good practice some days simply to pretend you are trimming the nails, just so your puppy will sit still and let you handle her feet.

Your Shih Tzu puppy has special nutritional needs to fuel her fast metabolism. She also has a small stomach, so she must eat small meals—several of them—and often! She does not have much body fat reserves. Her stomach is too small to hold enough food in a single meal to supply her daily caloric needs and support her growth, development, and activity level. She must have a diet specifically developed for small breed puppies that has a good balance of quality protein, fats, and carbohydrates to prevent hypoglycemia (low blood sugar)—a very common problem in Shih Tzu puppies. For more on puppy nutrition, see Chapter 6, "Shih Tzu Health and Nutrition," page 77.

HOME BASICS

Sample Vaccination Schedule

The following vaccination schedule should be considered only as a guideline.

Vaccine	1st inoculation Age	2nd inoculation Age	3rd inoculation Age	1st Booster Interval	Follow up Interval
Distemper	8 weeks	12 weeks	16 weeks	1 year	Every 2–3 years
Canine adenovirus-2 Hepatitis	8 weeks	12 weeks	16 weeks	1 year	Every 2–3 years
Parvovirus	8 weeks	12 weeks	16 weeks	1 year	Every 2–3 years
Rabies	12 weeks to 16 weeks (state laws vary)			1 year	Every 3 years (state laws vary)

Puppy Vaccination Chart

Shih Tzu puppies are tiny and very sensitive. Which vaccines to give your puppy, and when, are decisions you will make together with your veterinarian. Your veterinarian may separate the time intervals between vaccines by a few days or a few weeks, rather than give them all at one time. By spacing some of the vaccinations, your puppy's immune system may respond better and the chances of adverse reactions may be reduced.

Vaccination is a medical decision, not a calendar event. The type of vaccination, and when it is given, should be determined according to your puppy's lifestyle, age, health condition, past medical history, and potential risk of exposure. There are significant benefits, as well as some risks, associated with any vaccine.

CAUTION

When you take your Shih Tzu puppy to your veterinarian, do not coddle or baby her. Do not act protective. Do not act like you feel sorry for your puppy, or that you are worried. If you do these things you will teach your puppy to be afraid of her veterinarian and make her think she has something to worry about or fear. Be reassuring, yet matter of fact. Praise her for being brave and encourage confidence.

Chapter Five

Living with a Shih Tzu

Does your Shih Tzu act as though the world revolves around her? If so, she is acting just like a normal Shih Tzu! Some breeders have described Shih Tzu as "toys with an attitude." And you may have unknowingly contributed to that attitude by the way you treat your Shih Tzu. If you spend a lot of time cuddling your Shih Tzu and telling her how special she is, she may not understand every word you say, but she gets the gist, and she believes you! In your Shih Tzu's mind, *you* are her world—and *she* is the center of your universe. She wants to be the focus of all of your attention, all of the time.

It is very easy to spoil a Shih Tzu. They love to be pampered and they return affection with enthusiasm. At times it may easier to give in to them and let them have their own way, rather than engage in a war of wills. Give your Shih Tzu lots of socialization, supervision, and guidance. Kindly teach her the rules and limits. If you do, your Shih Tzu will prove to be one of the sweetest, most affectionate—and most obedient—dogs you will ever love. And one of the happiest, too!

Shih Tzu and Children

Shih Tzu are renowned for their outstanding disposition and sweet, gentle nature. They are good with children. Nevertheless, accidents sometimes happen when children and animals interact. So, for the well-being of the child and dog, here are some guidelines to help keep them both safe and injury free.

Safety Rules for Children

Safety is the top concern when it comes to children and Shih Tzu interactions. Set safety rules and make sure children follow them closely.

- Always be sure an adult is present to supervise interactions. (This is especially important for children under ten years of age.)
- Ask the owner for permission before you pet the dog.
- Approach the animal calmly and quietly. Do not startle or frighten her.

- Speak in a soft, gentle voice. Do not shout or yell.
- Petting the top of the head may be perceived as a threat, so gently pet under the chin instead.
- Do not grab, clutch, or hug the dog. (Children may squeeze too tightly and unintentionally hurt a Shih Tzu and provoke her to bite in self-defense.)
- Play calmly. Do not play rough, do not play tug-of-war, do not encourage or allow jumping, chasing, play biting, or nipping.
- Do not put your face up close to the dog's face and do not try to kiss the dog.
- Be careful where you walk so you do not to trip over the dog or step on her.
- Never tease a Shih Tzu.

Teach children to not put their face up close against your Shih Tzu's face. Children are naturally tempted to rub their cheeks across the soft fur and they often try to kiss animals, too. In addition to the obvious risk of possible disease spread from "kissing" animals (some germs and parasites can be spread between dogs and humans), trying to "kiss" a dog can startle the animal or

Breed Truths

A Shih Tzu is *not* for you if
- you want an outdoor dog;
- you want a rough and tumble play dog;
- you want a hunter, herder, retriever, or aggressive dog;
- you want a dog you can leave alone for long periods of time;
- you do not have a lot of time to spend with a dog;
- you do not have time or money for a high-maintenance dog;
- you cannot afford health care for a dog that might have special needs;
- you do not like dog grooming;
- you are allergic to dog hair and dander.

PERSONALITY POINTERS
Shih Tzu Pros and Cons

Pros	Cons
Affectionate and bonds closely with owner	High-maintenance dog that has special needs and is expensive to maintain
Intelligent	Can develop behavior problems if not properly socialized and trained
Eager to please	Obedience is not a Shih Tzu's strongest feature. Training can be challenging.
Friendly with other animals and with children	Not suitable for very young, small children, toddlers, and babies.
Small and portable, easy to crate train	Can be challenging to housetrain
Generally a sturdy, solid, healthy dog	The breed is predisposed to certain medical conditions. Shih Tzu are also prone to tooth and gum problems and need frequent dental cleaning.
Attractive with a beautiful coat that comes in a variety of colors	Shih Tzu require frequent, regular grooming
Does not eat as much as large breed dogs (however a quality diet is a must!)	Can be a picky eater or can be an eager eater with a tendency to overeat
Ideal for people who live in an apartment or small home, or people with a calm or sedentary lifestyle, or who live alone	Not suitable for people who want a dog to participate in extreme athletic sports, running, climbing, hiking, hunting, or swimming
Shih Tzu stay close to their owners and follow them everywhere	Easy to step on, trip over, or injure. Be careful where you walk, your Shih Tzu will always be underfoot!

be perceived as a threat. Shih Tzu are naturally friendly and not aggressive. But if accidentally injured, or startled, or frightened, your Shih Tzu could bite and inflict serious damage to a child's face.

It is very important that children learn the correct way to handle a Shih Tzu. Demonstrate the correct way to gently lift your puppy, by placing one hand under her hindquarters and the other hand under her chest and abdomen for support. Many children are too small, or have hands too small, to hold a puppy or an adolescent Shih Tzu without dropping her. It is safer for these children to sit on the floor, under adult supervision, and hold the puppy on their lap.

Teach children not to lift your Shih Tzu by her legs. She could be dropped or her limbs could be injured, dislocated, or broken. Children (and adults) should never restrain or lift a Shih Tzu by the nape of the neck (skin on the back of the neck). This is uncomfortable for the animal and she will try to escape. During the struggle, your Shih Tzu could be dropped and injured. Pulling on the skin at the back of the head or neck can also cause your Shih Tzu's eyes to bulge. In some cases, if the skin is pulled back too tightly, one or both eyes can proptose (be forced out from their sockets). Immediate veterinary care is necessary to put the eye back in place and to save the eye and vision.

Your Shih Tzu can teach the children in your life a lot about the joys of canine friendship and loyalty, as well as responsible pet ownership. Young children can participate in the animal's care, learning the importance of fresh water, good food, a clean home, and a kind heart. Older children can learn a lot about animal behavior, training, exhibiting, and grooming.

Shih Tzu and Other Pets

Your Shih Tzu will be interested in meeting all members of your family, including other household pets. She will probably be very friendly, right from the start, but the other animals in your home may not readily accept her—unless they are Shih Tzu, too. Shih Tzu love having other Shih Tzu join the family.

When you first bring your Shih Tzu home, make sure the introductions are done slowly and safely. For example, if you own another dog or a cat, don't expect them to be friends with your Shih Tzu immediately. Your other pets will be cautious and possibly jealous of the newcomer. A resentful cat can inflict serious injury on an unsuspecting dog, especially a tiny puppy. To prevent a cat scratch eye injury (common injuries suffered by dogs) or a bite wound, do not allow your Shih Tzu near your cat while you are away, and supervise them closely for compatibility when you are home.

If you have another dog in the home, remember that it may be jealous of the attention you are giving your new Shih Tzu. While a puppy will enthusiastically welcome the company of other animals, adult and older dogs can be sensitive and jealous. Be sure to watch older dogs closely so that they do not play roughly and accidentally injure the newcomer.

CAUTION

Do not introduce your Shih Tzu to the following household pets:

- small mammals (mice, rats, hamsters, guinea pigs, and other rodent pets)
- birds
- reptiles

Your Shih Tzu would not deliberately try to kill or eat your tiny pets. However, your puppy might play roughly with your smaller pets and unintentionally harm or kill them. Besides, small animals and birds sense danger. Your Shih Tzu would frighten and stress them if she approached their cage. Make sure the lid and door to your small pet's cage is securely fastened and place the cage where your Shih Tzu cannot find it.

A good way to start introductions in the family is to place your Shih Tzu in an area of the home where she is safe from other animals, but where they can observe and smell each other. For example, if you have an area near the kitchen or living room, you can place a barrier gate to prevent your Shih Tzu from running loose in the house until she adapts to her new environment and your other pets are used to her. Make sure the barrier has a mesh small enough to prevent escape or accidental injury. You may also put her in a crate for the first few evenings so that your other household animals can approach and investigate, but cannot harm her.

Remember to pay extra attention to your established pets so they are not jealous of your new Shih Tzu. Divide your attention among your pets and give them all their fair share of time and affection.

CAUTION

Cat claws can rupture a Shih Tzu's eyes and cause blindness. For added safety, and until your Shih Tzu and cat get along together, keep your cat's toenails trimmed or ask your veterinarian to apply a soft plastic protective covering on them, such as Soft Paws.

Shih Tzu and Obedience

Obedience training starts the first day you bring your Shih Tzu home and it continues throughout her entire life. Step by step, one lesson at a time, you teach your Shih Tzu the basic rules of canine etiquette and the simplest commands (*come, sit*). She learns the meaning of the word "no." Eventually you teach your Shih Tzu more difficult commands that could possibly save her life in times of emergency (*down, stay, heel off-lead*). She continually seeks your approval and praise for good behavior. She tries to understand and learn. She wants to please you. Keep the learning pace, and your expectations, reasonable.

As your Shih Tzu grows and matures, she will absorb more concepts and learn more lessons every day. There is so much to learn and remember: do not jump on people, do not bark incessantly, be gentle with children, don't chew on the furniture, go outside to eliminate, use a crate, behave in the car, walk on a leash without pulling—the list is endless. We may not realize it, but even the basic good behavior we expect of a Shih Tzu, and that we so often take for granted is, in reality, a tremendous amount for a dog to assimilate and retain.

It is only natural that your Shih Tzu will forget or make mistakes along the way. When she errs she just needs a gentle reminder to put her back on course, followed by lots of praise for good performance. The level of obedience and good manners that your Shih Tzu attains will depend on how much time you spend with her, how well she is socialized, your skills as a trainer, and your Shih Tzu's learning ability.

Shih Tzu Health

Shih Tzu are solid little dogs and with good care, they can live well into their teens. However, Shih Tzu are high-maintenance dogs that demand a lot of time and attention, frequent grooming, and regular health care. They also have special needs and are predisposed to certain medical conditions.

The best way to keep your Shih Tzu healthy is to prevent problems before they start. Give your Shih Tzu the best care and nutrition possible and take her for regular veterinary checkups, routine vaccinations, and laboratory tests (to identify health problems and parasites). Shih Tzu are also prone to tooth and gum disease and need frequent dental cleaning and polishing.

A very important part of canine health that has been seriously overlooked until recent years is canine "mental well-being." Just like people, when animals are stressed, illness can result. When you commit to the responsibilities of Shih Tzu ownership, keep in mind that your Shih Tzu's mental well-being is an important component of her overall health. For more information see Chapter Six, "Shih Tzu Health And Nutrition," page 77.

Are You Ready for a Shih Tzu?

When deciding on whether to bring a Shih Tzu into your home, take the time to consider all of the following.

Companionship: Your Shih Tzu wants to be with you as much as possible, a constant companion, at your side, in your arms, on your lap, craving love and attention non-stop. She does not like being left alone for long periods of time. Do you have lots of time to stay home and play with your dog? Do you have time to socialize and train her?

Long-Term Commitment: Shih Tzu have long life spans. Some can live up to 15 years or more. Are you prepared to take the necessary time, *every day*, for several years, caring for your Shih Tzu? Do you

Helpful Hints

Keep training sessions short, make them interesting, and always end on a positive note with lots of praise.

have the financial resources to care for her long-term, especially when she ages and will have special needs? Will you be there for your Shih Tzu throughout her lifetime?

Patience and Time to Socialize and Train: Are you patient? Are you compassionate and understanding? Shih Tzu are good-natured, vivacious, and intelligent. They have minds of their own and can be challenging to train. Shih Tzu have short attention spans, selective memories, and are easily distracted. Do you have the patience, perseverance, and time to tame and train your little "lion dog"? Note: Housetraining usually requires several refresher courses!

Housing: The Shih Tzu is a palace-dweller. For thousands of years her residences included such fancy locations as Imperial Palaces, castles, dignitaries' homes, and movie stars' mansions. Your cozy home is your Shih Tzu's palace. Can you offer her a safe haven, with safe play areas, a comfortable place to sleep, and secure *indoor* housing?

Exercise: Shih Tzu need daily exercise. Do you have a safe enclosure where your Shih Tzu can play? Do you have time to take your Shih Tzu on several daily walks and play lots of games? Can you give your Shih Tzu the exercise she needs to keep physically fit and in good health? Can you supervise your Shih Tzu at all times?

Supplies and Accessories: Do you have all the supplies you need to keep your Shih Tzu happy and healthy, such as lots of safe chew toys, an exercise pen, a soft bed, a crate, blankets, dishes, a collar or harness, leash, and grooming supplies?

Grooming: Shih Tzu have a lot of hair! Are you ready to set aside lots of time for regular grooming sessions to keep your Shih Tzu's skin and coat healthy? Can you afford to take your Shih Tzu to a groomer on a regular basis?

Veterinary Care: Have you selected a veterinarian for your Shih Tzu and

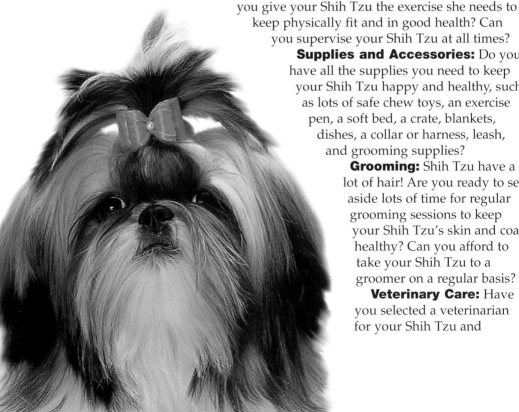

scheduled a physical examination for her? Are you prepared to pay for her health care, including vaccinations, microchip identification, and neutering (if indicated)? Do you have the financial resources to pay for emergency health care for your Shih Tzu, if needed?

Other Pets: Do you have time for a Shih Tzu and your other pets? Do you have a safe place to keep your Shih Tzu so that your other pets cannot harm or injure her?

Make sure the time is right to bring a Shih Tzu into your life. Wait until you have lots of free time to spend with your new dog to socialize, train, and care for her. If you are planning a vacation, getting married, expecting a new baby, moving, changing jobs, or are in the middle of the holiday season and entertaining visitors, you will not have enough time to spend with your Shih Tzu.

Breed Truths

Shih Tzu should always be housed indoors. They cannot tolerate harsh weather, especially heat. The brachycephalic face and long, flowing coat make it difficult for Shih Tzu to breathe in extreme temperatures. Shih Tzu must have good ventilation and fresh air. If you cannot house your dog indoors, do not even think of owning a Shih Tzu.

Chapter Six

Shih Tzu Health and Nutrition

S hih Tzu ownership is a very big—and a very long-term—commitment. From the moment you acquire your Shih Tzu, make a promise to her and to yourself that you will always give her the best care you possibly can, throughout her long life. Your healthy Shih Tzu can live fifteen years or longer. That means more time for you both to spend together!

Shih Tzu Health

It is easy to tell when a Shih Tzu is feeling great. She is bright-eyed, alert, active, inquisitive, and beautiful. If Your Shih Tzu is not acting normally, seems depressed, does not want to eat, is lethargic, losing weight, or has any other problems, call your veterinarian right away.

Is Your Shih Tzu Healthy?

Examine your Shih Tzu from her nose to her toes to make sure she is healthy. Her overall appearance should be outgoing, alert, and happy. Her body should be well-proportioned—not too thin, not overweight. She should have a natural stance, with her weight on all four feet equally, without favoring a foot. Hunched-up posture can mean back or abdominal pain. A drooping head may indicate neck, chest, or front limb pain. A head tilt may indicate ear pain, ear infection, parasites, or a nervous system problem.

Nose and Eyes

You Shih Tzu's nose should be free of discharge, mucus, or pus. A cold, wet nose is normal, but a dry nose does not indicate illness. Her eyes should be bright, clear, and free of discharge. Contact your veterinarian right away if you observe squinting, redness, irritation, excess mucus, or infection (green or yellow discharge) in or around your pet's eyes; or if the colored part of the eye (the iris) or the surface of the eye appears cloudy or hazy (possible cataracts or corneal edema). Shih Tzu may suffer from entropion, a rolling inward of the eyelids so that the lids and lashes rub on the surface of the eye. Shih Tzu can also inherit progressive retinal atrophy, an incurable hereditary disease that leads to blindness.

Mouth

Your Shih Tzu's gums should be healthy and bright pink, and her teeth should be free of tartar accumulation. Check for dental problems common in Shih Tzu, including retained deciduous (baby) teeth, missing teeth, malpositioned teeth protruding in gums, abnormal dental occlusion, or swelling of the jaw bone (caused by dentigerous cysts).

CAUTION

Keep your Shih Tzu clean and well groomed at all times. If your Shih Tzu's hair is matted or contaminated with fecal material under her tail, flies can lay hundreds of eggs in the matted hair. Maggots develop quickly in the damp, filthy, matted hair and rapidly invade, infect, and destroy body tissues.

Ears

Ears should be clean and free of bad odor. Check for dirt and wax buildup, and clean her ears regularly. Hair can accumulate near the ear canal and create a moist, warm environment ideal for bacterial and fungal growth. If your Shih Tzu's ears are sensitive, painful, reddened, have a foul odor, or if she shakes her head and scratches at her ears, contact your veterinarian right away. Your Shih Tzu could have an ear infection or parasites (such as mite or fleas), or a foreign object in her ear(s).

Skin

Your Shih Tzu's skin should be healthy and free of parasites, such as fleas, ticks, and mange mites. Her skin should not be dry, flaky, or greasy. Her coat should be well groomed and beautiful. If your Shih Tzu sheds excessively or her skin doesn't look healthy, consult your veterinarian.

Legs and Feet

Legs and feet should be pain free. Lameness can be difficult to detect if there is lameness in more than one limb. Lameness can be due to injury; bone and joint, muscular, or nervous system problems; a cut foot pad; or a foreign object. Feel the hind limbs. Bones that slip or pop may indicate patellar luxation (slipped kneecap).

HOME BASICS
How to Check your Shih Tzu's Vital Signs

Pulse: Place your fingers between your dog's ribs on the left side of the chest, behind the elbow, and feel the heartbeat OR place your fingers on the inside middle portion of either upper thigh, or in the groin area where the leg connects to the body. *Normal resting pulse is 80 to 180 beats per minute, depending on whether your Shih Tzu is at rest or has been very active.*

Temperature: Take your Shih Tzu's temperature rectally with a digital thermometer. Lubricate the tip of the rectal thermometer and gently insert it a distance of about one inch into your pet's rectum. Support your dog so she does not sit on the thermometer. *Normal Shih Tzu body temperature ranges from 100 to 102 degrees Fahrenheit.*

Circulation: Capillary refill time (CRT) is a good indicator of circulation. Press on the gums for a second with your finger. The gums should return to a bright pink color as the capillaries refill. *Normal CRT is 2 seconds or less.*

Respiration rate: Count the number of breaths your Shih Tzu takes in one minute. Respiration rate increases with excitement, heat, or difficulty breathing. *Normal respiration is 15 to 30 breaths per minute. Panting is more rapid.*

Hydration: Lift the skin over the shoulders and let go. The skin should quickly return to place. If the skin is slow to return, or remains "tented," then your Shih Tzu is dehydrated and needs fluids.

Check all four feet and between the toes for thorns and grass awns that cause pain and infection when hidden in the hair or tissues. Check for torn toe nails and overgrown nails, especially dewclaws. Check the nail beds for redness and infection. Trim nails regularly so they do not grow into the tissues of the footpads, causing pain, infection, and lameness.

Movement (Gait)
Your Shih Tzu should walk, trot, and run willingly and normally, without difficulty or limping. (Note: Shih Tzu gait can be hard to assess because they are small, close to the ground, have lots of hair, and move very quickly.) "Skipping" or "hopping" can be signs of patellar luxation.

Under the Tail
Check under the tail for signs of problems, such as swelling, hernias, anal sac impaction, abscesses, cysts, inflammation, diarrhea, and parasites (tapeworms). Prevent fecal material from becoming matted on the hair under the tail!

Sexual Maturity

Check Your Shih Tzu regularly for signs of estrus if she has not been spayed. If you have an intact male (not neutered), both of his testicles should be fully descended into the scrotum. One or both retained testicles (cryptorchidism) is common in toy breeds and is considered to be an inherited problem. The retained testicle(s) must be surgically removed or it can develop a Sertoli cell tumor (cancer) in later life. Retained testicles do not produce sperm and are usually abnormal in appearance.

Helpful Hints

Feel your Shih Tzu's body to be sure she is not too thin. All that hair can make her look bigger than she really is, so don't be fooled. *You should be able to feel your Shih Tzu's ribs slightly, but not see them.* The ribs should have a nice layer of flesh over them, but not a thick layer of fat.

Preventive Health Care

Preventive health care is the most important health care you can give your Shih Tzu.

There is a lot you can do to make sure your little lion dog stays as healthy as possible throughout her life. It is quick and easy to take a few moments every day to check your companion thoroughly while you play with her. Check her eyes, ears, nose, mouth, skin, feet, and area under the tail. Take note of her basic behaviors: eating, drinking, urinating, defecating, activity level, attitude, walking, running, and playfulness. Your observations can make all the difference between finding a problem in its early stage and treating it immediately and successfully, or finding a problem too late, when it has become serious.

FYI: Common Tests and Procedures

Test	Purpose	Procedures	Purpose
Fecal Test	Check for internal parasites: worms, protozoa (small amount of feces needed for test)	Vaccinations	Provide immunity against common canine viral and bacterial diseases
Heartworm Test	Check blood for heartworm disease (only a few drops of blood are needed for test)	Microchip Identification	Permanent form of identification in case pet is lost
Complete blood test and serum chemistries	Check blood for signs of anemia, infection, and check organ function and other body functions	Neuter	Surgery to remove reproductive organs to prevent reproduction and some types of cancer later life, and possibly improve some behavioral problems
Skin scraping	Check skin for mites	Deworming (vermifuge)	Treatment to eliminate internal parasites (worms)
Fungal culture	Check for fungi such as ringworm	Dewclaw removal	Surgical removal of small "thumb claw" on inside of front legs (usually done at 3 days of age but can be done at time of neuter)
Bacterial culture and sensitivity	Identify bacterial species and best antibiotic to treat the infection	Physical examinations	To ensure and monitor health

Your pampered Shih Tzu is a lucky pup! She lives during a time when most canine health problems and diseases can be prevented or treated. Malnutrition, severe parasitism, and bacterial and viral diseases used to be common canine killers. Dogs today benefit greatly from the superior nutrition offered in specially formulated and balanced diets. And, because Shih Tzu are housedogs, they share the same creature comforts that people enjoy. Finally, when help or guidance is needed to provide additional quality care, veterinarians, including board certified specialists, are there to assist with the latest in medical advances, technology, and prescription products.

Choosing a Veterinarian

Here are some guidelines to help you select the right veterinarian for your Shih Tzu.

- Ask the breeder, other Shih Tzu owners, dog trainers, groomers, and members of your local kennel club which veterinarians they recommend.
- Visit veterinary hospitals in your area. Meet the doctors and staff. Tour the facility.
- Inquire about the training and experience of the veterinarians, veterinary nurses, and staff. Ask if the nurses are licensed Registered Veterinary Technicians (RVT).
- Find a veterinary practice near you with convenient hours, including extended or weekend hours and 24-hour emergency service.
- Select a practice with doctors that work regular schedules so that the same doctor(s) see you and your Shih Tzu; there will be consistency and nothing will be overlooked in your pet's medical record or history.
- Ask about fees for services and payment arrangements. Veterinarians give price estimates for anticipated services. Payment is expected when service is rendered, unless payment arrangements have been made in advance.

Helpful Hints

Choose a veterinarian who is familiar with Shih Tzu; recognizes and understands their special breed characteristics, conditions, and needs; and who appreciates Shih Tzu as much as you do! Find a veterinarian before you need one and before a possible emergency situation. Take a test drive to the hospital so you know where to find it in advance of an emergency.

CHECKLIST

Contact your veterinarian immediately if your Shih Tzu has any of the following problems:

- ✔ Fever
- ✔ Pain
- ✔ Loss of appetite
- ✔ Lethargy
- ✔ Vomiting
- ✔ Diarrhea
- ✔ Discharge from the eyes
- ✔ Breathing problems
- ✔ Coughing, sneezing, wheezing
- ✔ Choking
- ✔ Lameness
- ✔ Head shaking
- ✔ Trembling
- ✔ Blood in the urine or feces
- ✔ Inability to urinate
- ✔ Severe constipation or inability to have a bowel movement
- ✔ Seizures
- ✔ Dehydration
- ✔ Weight loss

Vaccinations

Vaccinations (inoculations, immunizations) are the best method currently available to protect your Shih Tzu against serious, life-threatening diseases. Although there is not a vaccine available for every known canine disease, vaccines are available for some of the most common and deadly canine diseases. Your veterinarian will customize your pet's vaccine recommendations and schedule according to her lifestyle, age, health condition, past medical history, and risk of exposure.

The 2006 American Animal Hospital Association (AAHA) Canine Vaccine Guidelines updated recommendations divide vaccines into three categories:

1. **Core vaccines:** recommended (Canine Parvovirus, Canine distemper, Canine adenovirus-2 [hepatitis], Rabies)
2. **Non-core vaccines:** optional, depending on the dog's location and risk of exposure (Parainfluenza, *Bordetella, Borrelia burgdorferi* [Lyme Disease], *Leptospira*)
3. **Not recommended** (Canine coronavirus, *Giardia lambia*)

BE PREPARED! Common Canine Diseases That Can Be Prevented by Immunizations

Disease	Cause	Spread	Contagion	Signs
Distemper	Viral	Airborne, body excretions	Highly contagious, especially among young dogs	Difficulty breathing, coughing, discharge from nose and eyes, vomiting, diarrhea, dehydration, trembling, blindness, paralysis, seizures
Parvovirus	Viral	Contaminated feces	Highly contagious, especially among puppies	Diarrhea, dehydration, vomiting, heart problems and failure
Infectious canine hepatitis	Viral	Body excretions, urine	Highly contagious, especially among puppies and young dogs	Liver inflammation, jaundice, "blue eye" caused by fluid build-up; kidney damage, pain, internal bleeding
Leptospirosis	Bacterial	Urine contaminated in kennels or from wild animals	Highly contagious	Kidney and liver damage, jaundice, kidney failure, internal bleeding, anemia
Parainfluenza Bordetellosis Both cause "kennel cough"	Viral Bacterial	Airborne, sneeze and cough droplets	Highly contagious, especially in boarding kennels	Dry, hacking, continual cough of several weeks duration; may cause permanent damage to airways
Lyme Disease	Bacterial	Spread by the bite of an infected tick or contaminated body fluids		Swollen lymph nodes, lethargy, loss of appetite, joint swelling, lameness, heart and kidney disease
Rabies	Viral	Saliva (bite wounds)		Fatal, preceded by nervous system signs including paralysis, incoordination, and change in behavior

Treatments

Viral infections There is no treatment to kill a virus once infection has occurred. Treatment consists of supportive therapy such as fluids, antibiotics to control secondary bacterial infection, medications, and rest.

Rabies virus The rabies virus is fatal to dogs. A post-exposure treatment exists for humans infected with the rabies virus, but there is not one for animals.

Bacterial infections Bacterial infections are treated with antibiotics and supportive therapy as needed.

Parasite Control

Even though your Shih Tzu is an indoor dog, she can "acquire" several kinds of external parasites on her daily outings. Be on the lookout for fleas and ticks, especially during summer months. The number one cause of scratching and hair loss in dogs is caused by flea infestation. After every outing check your Shih Tzu's skin and hair closely and take time to brush out her coat.

Breed Truths

Shih Tzu are small and cannot tolerate internal parasite infestations as well as some larger breeds. Your Shih Tzu's health can rapidly deteriorate from the diarrhea, dehydration, anemia, irritation, and malnutrition that parasites cause.

Internal parasites (roundworms, hookworms, whipworms, tapeworms, and heartworms) and external parasites (fleas, ticks, ear mites, and mange-causing mites) can be killed and controlled with medications available as once-a-month tablets, topical applications, or by injection.

First Aid for Your Shih Tzu

The difference between life and death for your Shih Tzu could depend on how prepared you are. Prepare an emergency kit! Put all your supplies together *today* so you do not waste precious time trying to find what you need.

- Write down the doses for different medications and put the list in the kit so you can give the medicine without having to figure out the dose in the middle of a crisis.
- Make a copy of the emergency instructions in this book and put it in your first aid kit for easy reference.
- Keep your veterinarian's daytime and emergency telephone numbers near the phone. Keep an additional copy of emergency telephone numbers in the first aid kit.
- Keep the poison control center phone number in the first aid kit.

Put the first aid kit in a special place. When you travel with Your Shih Tzu, take the first aid kit with you.

FYI: Parasites That Affect Shih Tzu

Parasites	Transmission to Dogs	Transmission to Humans	Prevention
Internal			
Roundworms	Ingestion of eggs in feces of infected animals; transmitted from mother to pup *in utero* or in the milk	Accidental ingestion of eggs from contact with infected fecal material	Some parasiticides may be given to very young pups. Dewormings should be repeated as necessary.
Hookworms	Ingestion of larvae in feces of infected animals, direct skin contact with larvae	Direct skin contact with larvae in soil contaminated with feces of infected animals, accidental ingestion of larvae	Parasiticides
Whipworms	Contact with feces	No	Parasiticides
Tapeworms	Contact with fleas and feces, ingestion of fleas, eating raw meat (wild rodents)	Accidental ingestion of fleas and larvae	Parasiticides
Heartworms	Mosquito bite	No	Parasiticides
Protozoa	Contact with feces	Accidental ingestion of organisms in fecal material	Parasiticides
External			
Fleas	Allergy to flea saliva, skin irritation and itching, hair loss, transmission of tapeworms	Fleas may bite humans. Tapeworms also may be indirectly transmitted to people.	
Ticks	Transmission of Lyme Disease, skin irritation and infection	Humans can contract Lyme Disease from direct contact with ticks.	Always wear gloves when removing ticks from your dog to avoid contracting the disease.
Sarcoptic mange	Skin lesions and itching, hair loss	Sarcoptic mange can spread from pets to people by contact.	
Demodectic mange	Skin lesions, localized or generalized hair loss	No	

Use a Muzzle!

Dogs behave unpredictably when they are in pain or frightened. *For the safety of your pet and everyone involved, always muzzle your Shih Tzu before initiating emergency treatment, if your Shih Tzu is conscious!*

You can purchase a nylon muzzle from the pet store or you can make a muzzle from a strip of gauze about 18 inches long. Wrap the gauze around your Shih Tzu's muzzle, as close to the face as possible, and tie it securely under the chin. Take the ends of the gauze and tie them behind the head.

Shih Tzu ABCs: Airway, Breathing, Circulation

The most important things to check first in an emergency are

1. is the airway (trachea) unobstructed and open?
2. is your Shih Tzu breathing?
3. is the heart beating?

Note: Do not muzzle if your Shih Tzu is not breathing.

Airway Your Shih Tzu has a tiny throat and even tinier trachea (windpipe). Carefully open her mouth wide to check if anything is blocking the air passageway. Shih Tzu have delicate jaws, so be gentle. Use a pen light to look down the throat to make sure the trachea is not obstructed with a foreign object (food, toy particles, bones, or pebbles). Remove the object immediately to prevent suffocation. Do not push the object farther down the throat with your fingers. Forceps may be necessary to retrieve the object.

Breathing If your Shih Tzu is not breathing, you must act quickly and breathe for her. Open her mouth, remove any objects or debris, and clear away secretions. Pull her tongue out straight so it does not block the throat. Place your mouth over your Shih Tzu's nose and muzzle so that it makes a tight seal. Blow gently, but enough to make the chest rise. Do not blow too hard, or you can damage your dog's tiny lungs. Release so air can be expelled. Repeat this procedure every 5 seconds until your Shih Tzu breathes on her own. Check gum color often. The gums should return to a bright pink color if your dog is receiving enough oxygen.

Be careful! Only do this procedure if your Shih Tzu is unconscious or you may be bitten!

SHIH TZU

Cardiac If you cannot hear a heart beat, or feel a pulse, begin cardiopulmonary resuscitation (CPR) immediately so blood can circulate and bring oxygen to the lungs. Place your pet on her right side. Place both hands on top of each other and gently press your fingers on the left side of your Shih Tzu's chest, slightly above and directly behind the elbow. Continue to press and release at a rate of one to two presses every second. Remember to also breathe into the nostrils every five seconds. Continue CPR until your pet is able to breath on her own and you can feel a pulse.

What to Do In an Emergency

Important: If your Shih Tzu is suffering from any of the problems listed, consult your veterinarian immediately. This section is for emergency first aid only and is not a substitute for veterinary care.

Bite wounds Wounds to the head, neck, chest, and abdomen are serious. Wounds that penetrate the body cavity are life-threatening, especially if the lungs are partially collapsed or the internal organs are exposed. *Contact your veterinarian immediately regarding any bite wounds, and discuss the possible risk of rabies.*

To treat protruding body organs: cover organs with a warm, sterile, damp saline dressing. Do not push the organs back into the body. Rush your Shih Tzu to the hospital.

Cleanse other bite wounds, lacerations, tears, and puncture wounds with a disinfectant solution. Antibiotics, and possibly sutures, are necessary.

Bleeding or hemorrhage Excessive bleeding and pale gums are indicative of severe blood loss. Use gauze or a clean towel compress to apply firm pressure over the wound to stop the bleeding. If a large blood vessel in a limb has been severed, hemorrhage is life-threatening, so apply a tourniquet above the cut area. Loosen the tourniquet every 10 minutes to relieve pressure and allow circulation.

Bone fractures Symptoms include swelling, pain, and tenderness, abnormal limb position or movement, limping, and crepitation. Bone may remain under the skin or protrude up through it (open fracture).

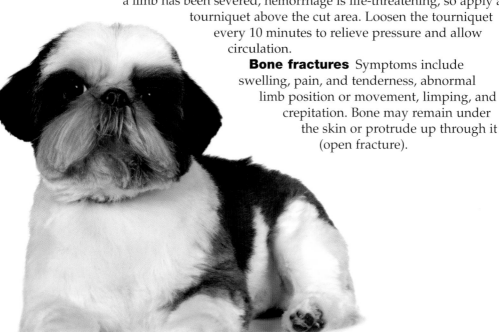

CHECKLIST

Supplies for Your First Aid Kit

The basic supplies and materials you need for your first aid kit can be purchased at your local pharmacy or from your veterinarian.

✔ Bandage scissors
✔ Small, regular, blunt-tipped scissors
✔ Thermometer
✔ Tourniquet (a strip of gauze will work)
✔ Tweezers
✔ Forceps
✔ Mouth gag (small wooden dowel will work)
✔ Hydrogen peroxide 3-percent solution
✔ Triple antibiotic ointment
✔ Roll of gauze bandage
✔ Gauze pads
✔ Telfa no-stick pads
✔ Sterile dressing and compresses
✔ Sterile saline solution
✔ Elastic bandage (preferably waterproof)
✔ Self-adhesive bandage (Vet Wrap type)
✔ Activated charcoal (for treatment of poisoning)

✔ Eyewash (sterile saline will work)
✔ Antihistamine capsules or tablets (diphenhydramine or chlorpheneramine)
✔ Antihistamine cream (diphenhydramine)
✔ Ophthalmic ointment (should *not* contain hydrocortisone)
✔ Cold compress (instant cold type)
✔ Small muzzle (Buy a comfortable nylon muzzle. If you do not have a muzzle, a gauze strip will work.)
✔ Blanket
✔ Paper towels
✔ Soap
✔ Sponge
✔ Exam gloves (vinyl)
✔ Penlight
✔ Flashlight
✔ Bottle water
✔ Electrolyte solution, such as Pedialyte
✔ Nutrical or other high sugar product, such as Karo syrup (corn syrup)
✔ Plastic bags
✔ Clippers (to shave wound areas)

If the bone is exposed, do not try to replace or cleanse it. Stop the bleeding and cover the wound with a sterile bandage to prevent further wound contamination. Place your pet on a soft bed, keep her calm, warm, and restrict her activity. Take her to your veterinarian immediately.

Burns Symptoms are red, swollen, inflamed, painful, and blistered skin. To treat thermal and electrical burns: Apply a cold, wet cloth or a cold pack to the area to cool the burn. Protect the burned area from the air with an ointment, such as Neosporin or aloe vera. To treat chemical burns: flush the burn profusely with water or saline to dilute and rinse the caustic chemical from the area. Do not allow your dog to lick the area or she will burn her mouth and esophagus with the caustic substance.

Choking Victims experience difficulty breathing or suffocation. Use a penlight or flashlight to look in the throat. Try to remove the object, using forceps, if possible. Do not push the object farther down the throat. A short

Breed Truths

Deadly Dangers: Dehydration, Hypoglycemia, and Hypothermia

The Shih Tzu's tiny size, high energy level, and fast metabolism makes it challenging for this toy breed to stay hydrated, nourished, and warm. *Dehydration, hypoglycemia, and hypothermia are the most common causes of death in small animals. Stressed, sick, very young, or very old Shih Tzu are especially fragile.*

wooden dowel—2 to 3 inches in diameter—inserted between the back molars, can serve as a gag to hold the mouth open.

Cuts To treat skin that is cut or lacerated, clip hair from around cut, clean the cut well with mild soap and water, dry and treat the cut with antibiotic ointment, and then bandage to keep clean. *Change the bandage daily.*

Eye injuries Symptoms of injured eyes include pain, squinting, tearing, sensitivity to light, redness, swelling, and dilated pupils. First place your Shih Tzu in a dark area. Contact your veterinarian immediately to relieve pain and increase the chances of saving the eye(s) and vision. If the eyes require flushing and rinsing, use a commercial, gentle, safe eyewash solution.

Dehydration To test for dehydration, pull up the skin at the nape of the neck. If it does not quickly return to normal position and remains "tented," the dog is suffering from dehydration. Offer water only if she is conscious. Do not force water if she is unconscious or too weak to drink or she may aspirate the water into her lungs. Keep a bottle of Pedialyte on hand for emergencies.

Heatstroke Symptoms include frantic, rapid breathing or struggling to breathe, bright red gums and bright red curling tongue, thick drool, vomiting, diarrhea, dehydration, and a rectal temperature of 105 to 110 degrees Fahrenheit. As the condition progresses, the body organs become affected, the animal weakens, goes into shock, then a coma, and dies. All of this happens rapidly.

Lower your pet's body temperature immediately by repeatedly wetting her down with cool (not cold) water. Check her body temperature every 3 minutes. When the temperature has dropped to 102 degrees Fahrenheit, stop wetting and monitor your pet closely. Do not give her water to drink until she is conscious. Take your Shih Tzu immediately to your veterinarian for follow-up care, including intravenous fluids and medications to treat shock and prevent cerebral edema (brain swelling).

Hypoglycemia (low blood sugar) Early signs of hypoglycemia may be

Helpful Hints

Do not give your Shih Tzu homemade salt or sugar mixtures without first consulting your veterinarian. In the wrong proportions, these will do more harm than good and further dehydrate your dog.

FYI: The 10 Most Common Poisonings in Dogs

- Ibuprofen (Advil, Motrin)
- Chocolate
- Ant and roach baits
- Rodenticides (rat, mouse, gopher bait)
- Acetaminophen (Tylenol)
- Pseudoephedrine in cold medicines (Pseudofed)
- Thyroid hormones
- Bleach
- Fertilizer
- Hydrocarbons (found in paint, varnish, furniture polish, lighter fluid)

subtle. The animal may sit quietly, but as blood sugar rapidly drops, symptoms become severe and include drowsiness, lethargy, inactivity, weakness, odd behavior, pale gums, lack of coordination, stumbling, and dilated pupils. If not treated immediately, seizures and death rapidly follow.

Do not try to force food or liquid into your Shih Tzu's mouth if she is unconscious. She can aspirate and choke to death. Instead, rub a sugar-rich substance on her gums, such as corn syrup. Wrap your Shih Tzu in a blanket and keep her warm. Check for signs of dehydration. Rush your Shih Tzu to your veterinarian immediately.

Hypothermia (low body temperature) Symptoms include shivering, lethargy, slow heart rate, slow respiration, coma, and death.

Warm your Shih Tzu *slowly!* Rapid heating, or overheating, causes serious problems. Wrap your Shih Tzu in a blanket. Fill plastic water bottles with warm (not hot!) water and place the bottles near, but not directly against, her body. Leave her head exposed and watch her closely. *Do not use an electric heating pad.* Check your pet's body temperature every five minutes. Do not let it to rise above 101.5 degrees Fahrenheit. Take your Shih Tzu to your veterinarian for follow-up care. *Never feed a Shih Tzu that is suffering from hypothermia. Wait until she is completely warmed.*

Insect stings produce swelling, redness, and pain. A severe allergic reaction can lead to facial and

FYI: Color Code for Gums

You can tell a lot about your Shih Tzu's health just by checking the gums.
- Bright pink: normal
- Red: inflammation, fever, heatstroke, possible poisoning
- Red specks or red spots: bleeding problems or infection
- Pale pink or white: anemia, hemorrhage or significant blood loss
- Blue, gray: insufficient oxygen delivery to the body
- Yellow: jaundice (icterus), liver problems
- "Muddy": very serious, near death in some cases
- "Tacky" or sticky to the touch: dehydrated

throat swelling and difficulty breathing. Pain, swelling, lethargy, vomiting, difficulty breathing, and lack of consciousness are all signs of a reaction.

Bees leave their stingers in the skin, but wasps and hornets do not. To treat bee stings: Remove the stinger by gently scraping it in one direction with a small, stiff business or credit card. If that fails, remove the stinger with tweezers, being careful not to squeeze the stinger, or more venom will be injected into the site. Apply a paste mixture of water and baking soda or an ice pack to the stung area to relieve pain.

To treat wasp stings: Apply vinegar to the area for pain relief. A topical antihistamine cream applied to the stung area can be beneficial. Sensitive animals can benefit from oral and topical antihistamines.

If the swelling worsens, contact your veterinarian immediately.

Poisoning Indications include restlessness, drooling, abdominal pain, vomiting, diarrhea, unconsciousness, seizures, shock, and death. *Contact your veterinarian immediately. Contact the poison control center.* If the poison came in a container (antifreeze or rodent poison), read the container label and follow the emergency instructions for treating poisoning. To induce vomiting, give ¼ to ½ teaspoon of 3-percent hydrogen peroxide. Use activated charcoal to dilute and absorb ingested poisons (available in powder, tablet, or capsule form from your veterinarian). All poisonings require veterinary care.

Seizures may be mild or severe, ranging from a mild tremor of short duration, to violent convulsions, chomping jaws, frothing at the mouth, stiffening of the neck and limbs, and cessation of breathing.

During a severe seizure, the animal is not conscious and can be hurt thrashing about on the floor. She may appear to be choking, but do not handle her mouth or you will be bitten. Try to prevent your Shih Tzu from injuring herself until the seizure has ended. After a seizure, your dog will be exhausted and disoriented, or dazed. Wrap her in a blanket to keep her comfortable, safe, and warm and take her immediately to your veterinarian.

Shock (resulting from a decreased blood supply to organs and tissue death) Symptoms include vomiting, diarrhea, weakness, difficulty breathing,

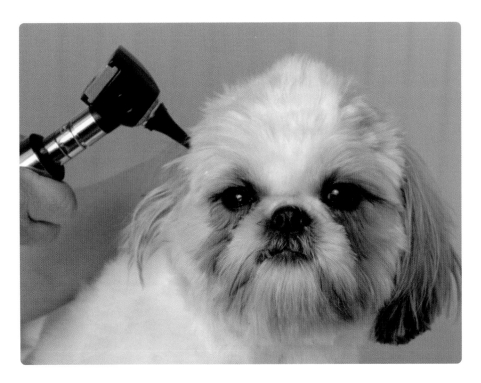

increased heart rate, collapse, and coma. Shock results in a rapid death unless immediate veterinary care—including fluid and oxygen therapy and a variety of medications—are provided.

Shih Tzu Disorders

Shih Tzu, like all breeds, are predisposed to certain disorders or medical conditions. Some problems are inherited and others may be congenital. Other types of problems may be acquired later in life.

Brachycephalic conditions: an elongated soft palate, small or pinched nostrils, and breathing difficulties.

Dental abnormalities: abnormal placement of teeth: misalignment, malocclusion; abnormal number of teeth: missing teeth, retained deciduous (baby) teeth; dentigerous (teeth bearing) cysts that cause bone and jaw lesions.

Ear conditions: Congenital deafness; infections (the dropped ear covers the ear canal, making a warm, moist environment for bacteria and yeast to grow), characterized by foul odor, waxy buildup, pain, and itching.

Skin problems: allergies: food, parasites (especially fleas); immune-related skin problems

Endocrine (hormonal) conditions

Bleeding disorders: slow blood clotting time (Von Willebrand's Disease)

Skeletal problems: Open fontanelle: failure of the "soft spot" on the skull to close completely by adulthood; Patellar luxation: the kneecap slips in and out of proper position due to a flaw in bone (femur) structure and weak ligaments (can be surgically corrected).

Eye Problems

Eye problems can occur at any stage of life and many conditions are hereditary. *All Shih Tzu should be checked annually by a Board Certified Veterinary Ophthalmologist and certified by the Canine Eye Registration Foundation.* Eye problems include:

- **Lagophthalmos:** inability to close the eyelids completely
- **Proptosis:** eye forced out of the socket, usually by trauma, and the eyelids close behind the eyeballs and shut off blood supply to the eyes. *This is an emergency that must be treated within minutes. Take your Shih Tzu to your veterinarian immediately!*
- **Distichiasis and trichiasis:** abnormal position of eyelashes on the margin of the eyelids, causing the eyelashes to rub against and irritate the surface of the eye, leading to ulceration and scarring of the cornea and eventual blindness

- **Ectopia cilia:** abnormal location of eyelashes. Instead of growing out from the eyelid margins, the eyelashes grow out from the conjunctiva, usually from the center area of the upper eyelid.
- **Entropion:** inward rolling of the eyelids, can cause eyelashes to rub on the cornea and cause corneal edema and other problems
- **Cataracts:** clouding opacity of the lens of the eyes that may cause partial or total blindness
- **Keratitis:** inflammation of the cornea (surface of the eye)
- **Keratoconjunctivitis ("dry eye"):** an abnormality of the composition of tears that causes corneal irritation, corneal ulceration, and blindness
- **Retinal detachment:** the retina becomes separated from the back of the eye, leading to blindness
- **Progressive retinal atrophy (PRA):** degeneration of the cells of the retina, starts out as "night blindness" (difficulty seeing at night) and later develops into total blindness. PRA is an inherited disorder.

Kidney Problems

In addition to stone formation in the kidneys or urinary bladder, renal dysplasia is a serious, common hereditary condition in the Shih Tzu. Renal dysplasia is a failure of the kidneys to fully develop. Symptoms of the disease vary from severe to slight and include excessive drinking and urinating, small size and weight, lethargy, lack of appetite, and overall poor condition. Some animals die at an early age, others may live longer and slowly debilitate. Shih Tzu that are mildly affected may live a relatively normal life and pass the genetic condition on to their offspring. Diagnosis is made by a kidney biopsy. Ultrasound imaging can detect the size and shape of the kidney and laboratory tests can help determine degree of severity.

There is a DNA test available to identify Shih Tzu that are genetic carriers of the disease. All Shih Tzu should have a DNA test for renal dysplasia *before* they are used for breeding purposes. Information on DNA testing can be obtained from the American Shih Tzu Club (see Information). *Shih Tzu that have renal dysplasia or are genetic carriers of the disease should never be used for breeding.*

Liver Problems

Portal systemic shunt is a circulatory abnormality. Embryonic blood vessels that carried oxygenated blood from the placenta to the fetus do not close within a few days of birth, as they should. They remain open so that blood that would normally be directed to the liver for detoxification is instead shunted through the embryonic vessels and bypass the liver. Hepatic (liver) detoxification is necessary to prevent accumulation in the body of toxic substances such as ammonia.

Toxins build up in the body, causing a wide range of symptoms. Signs of portal caval systemic shunt include chronic illness, urinary crystals and stones (ammonium biurate), increased thirst, weight loss, vomiting, diarrhea, salivation, and neurologic (nervous) symptoms. Affected animals may have seizures, circle aimlessly, press their heads against objects, or suffer from dementia.

Portal systemic shunt appears to be an inherited disorder in Shih Tzu and although it may be temporarily managed with a low protein diet, the animal will eventually die of the disease unless the shunt is closed surgically. Surgery is difficult and not always successful.

Animals with relatives known to be affected with portal shunt system should not be used for breeding.

Shih Tzu Nutrition

Quality nutrition is the key to your Shih Tzu's overall good health. Every aspect of your Shih Tzu's health and well-being hinge on what you feed her. Fortunately, nutrition is one aspect of your pet's health over which you have full control! Don't cut corners when it comes to feeding your Shih Tzu. Proper, balanced, complete nutrition will strongly impact her health, development, coat quality, mental acuity, and life span.

Your Shih Tzu's diet will need to be adjusted and modified at different stages in her life. When she is a puppy, she will need a dog food that provides complete and balanced nutrition for puppy growth and development. As she reaches adolescence, her dietary requirements may lessen or increase, according to her individual needs, genetics, activities, environment, and metabolism. When your Shih Tzu is an adult, she will have greater nutritional requirements if she is active, doing obedience or agility work, on the show circuit, or pregnant or lactating, than she would have if she were sedentary. Finally, as your pet ages, or if she becomes sick or is recovering from an illness, she will need a diet based on her health condition and special needs.

Environment plays an important role in dietary requirements. Your Shih Tzu is a housedog. She does not have the high caloric requirement of dogs that live in cold weather or working or hunting dogs.

Finally, genetics can influence a dog's caloric requirements. If some members of your Shih Tzu's family have difficulty maintaining a good weight, this may be an inherited tendency and you will have to make a special effort to closely monitor her food sources and consumption. If your Shih Tzu is prone to genetic problems, such as renal disease, she will need a special diet to accommodate her health problem and lessen stress on her kidneys or other body organs.

What to feed and how much to feed are decisions you will make as your Shih Tzu changes throughout life. For each of your Shih Tzu's life stages, you should consult your veterinarian to learn which type of dog food would be most beneficial and how much to feed based on her caloric needs at that time.

Dog Food

There are countless brands and types of commercial dog foods on the market. Do not feed your Shih Tzu an inferior dog food that is not nutritionally balanced simply because she likes the flavor. Often the tastes and smells that your dog likes are due to food additives and artificial flavorings and not due to nutrients.

The amount you should feed your Shih Tzu depends on her stage of development, activity level, and environment, in addition to the quality of the food you give her. High-quality dog food is easily digested, so a smaller amount is needed than if you feed a mediocre diet filled with bulk and fiber material that cannot be digested.

Dog Food Labels

The following is a breakdown of what you will find listed on dog food labels.

Ingredients Everything that is mixed together to make a specific dog food. Ingredient lists tell nothing about the *quality* or the *digestibility* of the ingredients, which may or may not have nutritional value. Fat, proteins, carbohydrates, vitamins and minerals are nutritional components of dog food. Non-nutritional ingredients include food additives, artificial coloring, artificial flavorings, and food preservatives. Labels list ingredients in decreasing order of preponderance. Manufacturers may use the same types of ingredients, but they vary in quality and digestibility. *You cannot rely solely on the comparison of ingredient labels to select dog food.*

Nutrients Substances necessary for life's processes. Some nutrients produce energy (sugars, amino acids, and fatty acids). Some nutrients do not produce energy, but are required for life (water, oxygen, vitamins, and minerals).

HOME BASICS
Dog Food Decisions

There are so many dog food brands and types on the market, selecting the best one for your Shih Tzu can be a challenge. Here are some guidelines.

- Select a high-quality food that contains quality protein (meat) and fat.
- Choose a dog food with rice, wholesome grains, or potatoes for carbohydrate sources. Corn causes food allergies, itchy skin, and excessive weight gain in some dogs.
- Feed dry food whenever possible. Dry food is more filling and keeps teeth and gums healthier by helping to reduce plaque buildup. Canned food is more expensive and less nutritious by weight. You are paying mostly for water, which makes up 70 percent or more of the canned contents. Semi-moist food should be reserved for occasional treats. It is high in sugar, expensive, and lower in quality.
- Avoid raw foods. They can contain dangerous bacteria such as *E. coli* and *Salmonella*, as well as small bone particles that could cause choking.
- Feed only healthy treats, such as raw vegetables, dried preservative-free "jerky" chicken breast, bits of cheese, and bits of lean meat. Keep treats to a minimum.

The type and amount of nutrients contained in a dog food mixture make up the nutrient profile.

Nutritional adequacy The American Association of Feed Control Officials (AAFCO) requires dog food companies to demonstrate the nutritional adequacy of their products, either by feeding trials, or by meeting the AAFCO Nutrient Profile. Dog food manufacturers must make a statement about the nutritional adequacy of all their products (except treats and snacks), such as "complete and balanced nutrition."

Proteins Proteins, and protein quality, are the most important health factors in a Shih Tzu's diet. Protein comes from plant or animal sources. High-quality animal source proteins are better for dogs than plant source proteins because they provide a better balance of amino acids. Do not confuse a high percentage of protein in the diet with high-quality protein. Animal source proteins in commercial dog foods include beef, chicken, turkey, duck, lamb, fish, and eggs. Read the label and look for "meat," "meal,"and "by-products." Meat: muscle and skin, with or without bone; Meal: protein source is ground up into particles; By-products: heads, feet, guts, and bone.

Fats Fats are important components of a Shih Tzu's diet and influences skin and coat condition. Fats add flavor to food, provide energy, and play a major role in digestion and the assimilation of fat-soluble vitamins A, D, E,

and K. Various fats (animal fat, vegetable oils, olive oil, fish oils) have different effects on the body and many are used for therapeutic remedies.

Carbohydrates Carbohydrates are sugars, starches, and fibers. They are an inexpensive source of energy. *Researchers have not yet determined the exact amount of carbohydrates required in the canine diet, yet carbohydrates make up the major portion of today's commercial dog foods.* Dog food carbohydrates are usually corn, corn meal, rice, or a combination of grains. Dogs cannot digest fiber, so it is used in many dog foods to maintain dry matter bulk and for weight-reduction diets.

Vitamins Vitamins are classified as fat-soluble (vitamins A, D, E, and K) or water-soluble (all the B vitamins and vitamin C). Dogs make their own vitamin C and do not require vitamin C supplementation in their diet.

Minerals Minerals are necessary for life-sustaining daily activities, such as skeletal growth and development, and muscle and nerve function. Minerals required for life include calcium, phosphorus, sodium, potassium, magnesium, zinc, selenium, iron, manganese, copper, and iodine.

Additives and Preservatives Substances added to dog food to improve or enhance color, flavor, and texture, and to extend product shelf life. Additives, such as antioxidants, are added to dog food to help keep fat in the food from becoming rancid over time. Other additives are used to slow down bacterial and fungal growth.

Supplements If you feed your Shih Tzu a high-quality dog food, nutritional supplementation is usually unnecessary. By supplementing the diet with other products, nutritional balance can be disrupted. Consult your veterinarian about any form of supplementation before adding it to your Shih Tzu's diet. An overdose of vitamins is just as dangerous as a vitamin deficiency, and can cause serious medical problems. In addition, minerals should be provided in a balanced ratio. Excessive supplementation of minerals can lead to serious medical conditions.

Shih Tzu Weight

The best way to know if your Shih Tzu is eating the right amount is to check her overall physical condition and appearance *every day*. *You should be able to feel the ribs, but not see them.* Weigh her once a week, if possible, and not less than once a month. If you notice any weight loss or gain, consult your veterinarian.

To weigh your Shih Tzu, hold her and stand on the scale. Now weigh yourself alone. Subtract your weight from the combined weight and the difference is your Shih Tzu's weight. Another option is to purchase a basket scale designed to weigh small animals. You can also use your veterinarian's hospital scale. Adult Shih Tzu should weigh 9 to 16 pounds.

Helpful Hints

If your Shih Tzu is selective about what she eats, you can flavor her dry food with bits of salmon, chicken, lean meat, or sprinkle a little low-fat cheese on her food. You can moisten her dry food with the liquid from canned salmon.

Feeding Shih Tzu Puppies

Shih Tzu puppies are active individuals that burn off calories quickly. Their initial growth phase is during the first six months of life, although technically they are still puppies until 8 to 12 months of age, or when they reach puberty. Your Shih Tzu puppy has a small stomach and a high metabolism. Feed her four to six times a day to prevent hypoglycemia. When your puppy's growth and development begin to slow down, at about 12 to 20 weeks of age, you can feed her four meals daily. When she is about 6 months of age, she can be switched to an adult feeding schedule of two meals daily, twelve hours apart. After the evening meal, a leisurely stroll before bedtime will help your Shih Tzu sleep more comfortably.

Be sure to consult your veterinarian to be certain this feeding schedule matches your Shih Tzu's specific needs.

Obesity

Obesity is a form of malnutrition in which there is a ratio of too much fat to lean body tissue. We usually think of malnutrition as being a shortage of food, resulting in a thin, starving individual. However, malnutrition means bad nutrition (from the French word "mal" for "bad"). Malnutrition refers to all aspects of unbalanced nutrition, whether it is too little, or too much.

The most effective way to prevent your eager eater from becoming over-weight is to closely monitor her food intake and don't overfeed her. *Overeating is the most common cause of obesity in dogs.*

Water

Water is the most important of all nutrients. Your Shih Tzu loses body water throughout the day, in the urine and feces, by evaporation, panting, drooling, and footpad sweating. She loses water faster in warm weather and when she is active. Make sure fresh water is available at all times to avoid dehydration and illness.

Monitor how much water your Shih Tzu drinks every day. She should drink at least one ounce of water per pound of body weight per day. If your Shih Tzu is active, the weather is warm, or if she is pregnant or lactating, her water intake will be much greater.

Helpful Hints

Shih Tzu readily drink from a sipper tube and water bottle. Clean and fill the bottle every day and measure exactly how much your Shih Tzu drinks in a 24-hour period.

If your Shih Tzu is continually thirsty or drinks more than usual, it may be a warning sign for possible illness, such as diabetes or kidney disease. If she is not drinking much, she can become dehydrated and develop health problems. Sufficient water intake is especially important in older animals, because they often have reduced kidney (renal) function. If your Shih Tzu is drinking excessively, or not drinking enough, contact your veterinarian immediately. She could have a serious health problem.

10 **Questions** About Your Dog's Health Care & Nutrition

1 **What should I feed my Shih Tzu?** Feed your Shih Tzu the same food she was fed at the breeder's, or a top-quality food developed for toy or small breeds, or a food recommended by your veterinarian depending on your pet's requirements. Feed your puppy a quality puppy food. Feed your adult a diet designed for adult small breeds. If your Shih Tzu has special needs, food allergies, or is overweight or underweight, she may need a prescription diet.

2 **How much should I feed my Shih Tzu?** Feed your Shih Tzu according to her age, health, and activity level. Weigh your Shih Tzu and determine whether she is the right weight or too thin or too heavy, then adjust her food intake accordingly. Ask your veterinarian for advice.

3 **How often should I feed?** Feed your Shih Tzu puppy small, frequent meals to prevent her from having low blood sugar. When your Shih Tzu is a tiny puppy, six or more small meals daily may be necessary. When she is a growing adolescent, she may need three to four meals daily. Adult Shih Tzu usually do well on two to three meals a day, unless they have a very high activity level and a higher caloric requirement.

4 **Do I need to supplement?** If you are feeding your Shih Tzu a top quality food, supplements are usually not necessary. In fact, supplements can upset the overall nutritional balance of the food you are feeding. Over supplementation of vitamins and minerals can be harmful.

5 **Should I feed my Shih Tzu treats?** Feed only a very small amount of treats and use them mostly as training rewards. Feed healthy treats that are low calorie and free of preservatives and artificial flavorings, such as 100-percent dried chicken, duck, or turkey breast strips, available from your pet store. Do not feed leftovers from your table!

6 **My Shih Tzu is strictly a house dog. Does she really need vaccinations?** Even though your Shih Tzu lives indoors, every time she goes for a walk, or to the park, is boarded, or encounters other dogs, she is at risk for contracting deadly diseases. She will not be protected against these diseases unless she is vaccinated. Rabies is a serious disease that is fatal to humans and animals, and rabies vaccination is required by state law.

7 **Why does my Shih Tzu scoot around on her bottom sometimes? What should I do?** There are many reasons your Shih Tzu might scoot on her bottom. They include parasites (worms), perianal inflammation and itching, feces stuck to the hair around the anus, and anal sac problems. If your Shih Tzu is a scooter, take her to your veterinarian to have the problem diagnosed and treated.

8 **My Shih Tzu has bad breath and plaque buildup on her teeth. What can I do?** Shih Tzu are prone to dental and gum disease caused by bacteria, plaque, and tartar buildup that causes bad breath and leads to periodontal disease and other serious illnesses. Ask your veterinarian to clean and polish your Shih Tzu's teeth. Polishing smoothes dental surfaces and slows plaque buildup. After your Shih Tzu's teeth are clean, you can brush her teeth at least once a week. Your Shih Tzu will still need to have routine dental cleaning, but not as often as she would if you didn't brush her teeth regularly.

9 **My Shih Tzu has some hair discoloration and staining near the inside corners of her eyes. What causes this and what can I do about it?** Hair staining near the eyes is usually caused by excess tearing (caused by hair and other irritants in the eyes), sometimes in conjunction with impaired tear drainage (blocked tear ducts) and other problems (lower lip entropion or apposition to eye). This condition is common in Shih Tzu and other dogs with prominent eyes that are surrounded by lots of hair, and that have a short muzzle. Veterinary ophthalmologists believe the red-brown hair staining is due to porphyrins in the tears. The tearing causes moisture buildup in the hair and skin around the eyes, which leads to bacterial and yeast growth and dermatitis (inflamed, reddened skin). Keep your dog's eyes wiped clean and dry daily. Consult your veterinarian to rule out serious eye problems. Staining is difficult to eliminate completely. Your veterinarian can recommend a safe product for your Shih Tzu when the exact cause of your Shih Tzu's excess tearing is identified.

10 **Sometimes I notice a foul odor under my Shih Tzu's tail. What is that and what can I do about it?** All dogs have a pair of anal sacs located on each side of the inside of the rectum. They contain a bad smelling brown liquid that is usually emptied during defecation. Sometimes the sacs become impacted and need to be manually expressed (emptied) by a veterinarian or groomer. Consult your veterinarian to make sure your Shih Tzu's anal sacs are not impacted, infected, abscessed, or ruptured.

Chapter Seven

Training and Activities

To be a good canine citizen and an acceptable member of society, your Shih Tzu must learn some basic manners. The key to success is to make training fun. Shih Tzu have short attention spans, especially Shih Tzu puppies. They bore quickly if subjected to long training sessions with repetitive lessons. Shih Tzu prefer to play! It is up to you to convince your little canine that training is a game.

A small food reward now and then is a great way to gain your Shih Tzu's attention and hold it long enough to teach her. Don't give her a food reward every time she does something right. Keep her guessing, so you can hold her attention longer, but give her rewards often enough that she doesn't give up on them. Always give her verbal praise and caresses when she accomplishes even the smallest of feats. Eventually your Shih Tzu will do what you ask her to do because she *wants* to please you. Keep in mind that your Shih Tzu cannot do what you ask her to do until she completely understands the command and has mastered it. Be patient. Start with the simplest commands, such as *sit* or *come*, and take the necessary time to thoroughly teach each command before you start to teach her a new one.

Shih Tzu training starts the moment you bring your new little friend home. Start with simple, basic lessons. A basic puppy class, or dog training class, is one of the most effective ways to begin basic obedience training and to teach your puppy to pay attention. Puppy classes are also a great way to socialize your puppy.

There are as many different training techniques as there are dogs and trainers. Before you sign up for a puppy class, ask to visit a class while it is in session so you can decide if you, your Shih Tzu, and the trainer will make a good team. Shih Tzu are sensitive dogs that respond to positive, fun training techniques. Harsh training techniques can ruin a Shih Tzu and make her fearful for life. Make sure that the techniques the trainer is using are appropriate for a Shih Tzu.

Training Commands

Name

Your Shih Tzu must first learn her name so you can get her attention to teach her. Start by calling her name when you want to play with her or when you feed her. It won't take her long to associate her name with the idea that you have something fun or tasty planned for her. Make learning her name a game. Sit on the floor and have a friend sit on the floor opposite you, just a few feet away. Call your Shih Tzu. When she comes to you, give her a small food treat. Next, have your friend call your puppy and reward her when she comes. Continue to alternate: first you call your puppy and then your friend calls your puppy. Gradually increase the distance between you and your friend. Be sure to give your puppy a little food reward and lots of praise when she responds and stop the game *before* she tires of it!

Come

Say your puppy's name to get her attention. Then say, "Come." In the beginning, use small tidbits as a reward to entice your puppy to come to you and give her lots of praise. Over time, decrease the frequency of food rewards, but always give lots of enthusiastic praise. Your puppy will quickly learn to come to you when called, purely for the attention you give her. Of course, you should still surprise her with a food reward now and then. Keeping her guessing is a good way to keep her attention!

Sit

The *sit* command is the easiest of all commands to teach your Shih Tzu. With some patience and consistency, your puppy will probably get the general idea and learn to *sit* in just a few training sessions.

Start by holding a small piece of food over her nose and raising your hand over her head. As your Shih Tzu's head goes up to follow the tidbit, her hindquarters will naturally drop down into a *sit* position. In the beginning, you may have to apply gentle pressure on the rump to help her get the right idea. The moment your puppy is in a sitting position, say "Yes!" (or click) and give her the treat. When you are ready to release her from the command, say "okay." When your puppy has learned this action, introduce the word "sit."

Helpful Hints

The keys to successful Shih Tzu training are
- be consistent, kind, and patient;
- keep training sessions brief;
- make training fun and interesting;
- give your Shih Tzu a food reward and lots of praise the moment she does the right thing;
- do not reward your Shih Tzu if she does not do what you asked her to do;
- always end training sessions on a positive note, right after your ShihTzu has done something right.

Placing your hand lightly on your Shih Tzu's nose will help prevent her from jumping up in excitement to grab the treat from you. Keep the treat protected in your hand and do not let your puppy have it until she is seated. As your puppy learns this command, teach her to remain in a sitting position for more than a few seconds. Gradually teach her that she must learn not to get up from the *sit* until you give her the release word, "okay" or "free!"

As training progresses, you may wait longer intervals before giving her the tidbit and eventually replace the food reward with praise.

Helpful Hints

To find a good puppy training class, join a local dog club and ask other Shih Tzu owners which trainers they recommend. Your breeder and veterinarian can also give you recommendations.

Down

Teach your Shih Tzu to lie down by starting from a sitting position. Place your puppy in front of a wall so that she cannot scoot backward. Because your puppy is so small and short, it is difficult to stand and bend over to train her. Either kneel down alongside her, on her right side, facing the same direction, or sit in front of her.

While your puppy is in a sitting position, show her that you have a food reward and slowly lower it so that she must point her nose to her chest. Continue to lower the treat to the ground and rest your hand lightly on her shoulders to guide her into position. If necessary, gently pull her legs out in front of her so she must drop into position. The moment your Shih Tzu is in the *down* position, say "yes!" or click, and give her the treat. Hold your puppy gently in the *down* position for a few moments, so she knows she must remain in that position, then give her the release word "okay" and let her go.

As your puppy masters this command, introduce the word "down" and use a palm down, downward motion of your hand, to signal the *down* command. As with other commands, you will eventually replace the food reward with praise alone.

Stay

Stay is a tough command for Shih Tzu. They want to be the center of attention and where all the activity is. Up until now you have been asking your Shih Tzu to come to you and to remain with you. Now you will be asking her to remain in place while you walk away or leave. At first she will be confused. It won't make a bit of sense to her unless you train her very carefully and patiently.

Don't try to teach your Shih Tzu to *stay* until she has learned the *sit* and *down* commands very well. When you first start training your Shih Tzu to *stay*, do not expect her to stay in place for more than a few seconds. It will take several lessons before she will *stay* for an extended time, but it is worth every minute of those lessons. *Stay* is a command that could potentially save your pet's life in case of emergency or danger.

There are a few ways to teach your Shih Tzu *stay*. You can teach the command in the *sit* or *down* position. Select a training method that you prefer and stick with it. Do not switch between methods.

Method 1: Some trainers recommend starting with your dog in the *down* position. While placing your hand firmly on top of your Shih Tzu's shoulders, tell her to *stay*. For the first few training sessions, try to teach your Shih Tzu to remain in place with your hand on her shoulders for 15 to 30 seconds, then give her lots of praise and a food reward.

For the next several lessons, make your Shih Tzu lie down and tell her to stay, then slowly back away from her about 3 feet and wait 30 seconds. If your Shih Tzu jumps up to run to you, gently return her to her assigned place and tell her to *stay*, while simultaneously keeping your hand on her shoulders.

After your Shih Tzu has learned to stay in place for 30 seconds with you seated a few feet in front of her, begin to lengthen the time period as well as your distance from her. If she starts to leave her designated spot, tell her to *stay* and raise your hand with the palm facing her. Your Shih Tzu will eventually associate the word "stay" with the hand signal and learn to remain in place until you give her the release word "okay"! Give her a food reward and lots of praise.

Method 2: Place a buckle collar (not a choke collar) on your Shih Tzu and attach it to a leash. Hold the leash, say your Shih Tzu's name, and tell her "sit" or "down." When she obeys, say "yes!" (or click) and give her a treat. Place a treat on the ground, a short distance in front of your puppy. When she tries to approach it, gently restrain her with your hand on her chest, or gently hold her in place with the leash and collar, and say "stay." Make her *stay* for a few seconds, then give the release signal, "okay," and let her have the treat. Slowly increase the length of the *stay*, and your distance from your Shih Tzu, little by little, over several weeks' time.

Your Shih Tzu may become very bored with the *stay* command, so keep training sessions to only a few minutes. End while she is still having fun and is enthusiastic. Be sure to bring the training session to a close immediately after one of the times she has done what you have asked of her, even if she did not do it perfectly.

Leash Training

After you have trained your puppy to come when called and to follow you around the house or yard, you are ready to begin leash training. Begin by attaching a light line, such as string or yarn, to her harness or collar, and allow her to drag the line behind her and to play with it. Encourage your Shih Tzu to follow you with the string dragging along. When she has become accustomed to the string, replace it with a very light leash. (A show lead is ideal.) Your puppy will quickly adapt to the leash dragging on the ground behind her. At that point you can hold the leash and walk with your puppy. Give her food rewards to entice her to follow or walk with you. Make it a game! If your puppy protests and pulls against the leash, do not scold or drag her. Talk to her to distract her and call her to you and reward her. Make sure she understands she is being rewarded for coming to you and walking with you, and not for struggling against the leash.

In the beginning, the distance you walk with your puppy should be short, maybe just halfway across the living room or partway across the backyard. With patience and consistency, your Shih Tzu will be following along on the leash in no time. She may weave a bit, or run a little ahead, or drop behind for a moment, but she will have the general idea. Once she reaches this level in her leash training, you can begin to work on fine-tuning her to *heel* close by your side on a loose lead.

Never leave your Shih Tzu alone or unsupervised while she is wearing a collar or attached to a leash.

Never tie your Shih Tzu to any objects.

Grooming Training

Grooming is so important to Shih Tzu that grooming training deserves special discussion. Begin grooming training immediately, while your Shih Tzu is still a young puppy. Begin by placing your puppy on your lap and caressing her head, face, and ears in a soothing, calming manner. Alternately pick up and hold each one of her feet. Make it a pleasant experience. Then gently place a soft brush on her back. At first your Shih Tzu will want to examine the object or try to chew on it. Once the curiosity has passed, try to gently and lightly brush her back. As your puppy accepts this contact, you may proceed to the top of her head, then her legs, and finally her tail. Continue to also rub her belly and scratch her ears now and then.

Most Shih Tzu love to be groomed; however, if your puppy objects to light brushing in the very beginning, don't stop. Talk to her cheerfully and continue to brush her lightly with a soft brush. If you stop grooming when your puppy protests, that will only reinforce her behavior. Be gentle, kind, and consistent in your training and always end on a positive note.

Keep the first training sessions very short, three minutes or less, and end them while your puppy is still enjoying the attention. Give a small food reward to signal good behavior and the end of the grooming session.

Table Training

Before you can groom your Shih Tzu on the table, she must be trained to sit, lie down, and stand quietly on a table, which means she must already have learned how to sit, lie down, and stand on the ground!

The key to success is to be gentle and patient, yet firm. Start by placing a rubber nonslip mat on the tabletop. Cover the mat with a towel and stand your dog on the mat.

If your Shih Tzu is just a puppy, begin by making her *sit* on the table. If she has already learned *sit* well on the ground, she will *sit* on the table.

Your Shih Tzu puppy won't realize that she is high off the ground, so make sure to keep a good hold on her at all times so she doesn't accidentally fall off the grooming table.

When your puppy is calm and still, gently brush her with a soft brush. At this point don't worry about brushing out every knot and tangle. Just work on getting her accustomed to being brushed while sitting on the grooming table.

Most Shih Tzu lie down and stand for grooming. In future training sessions, you can encourage your puppy to lie down on the grooming table so you can brush her. Eventually you will ask her to lie calmly on her side so you can brush different parts of her body in sections.

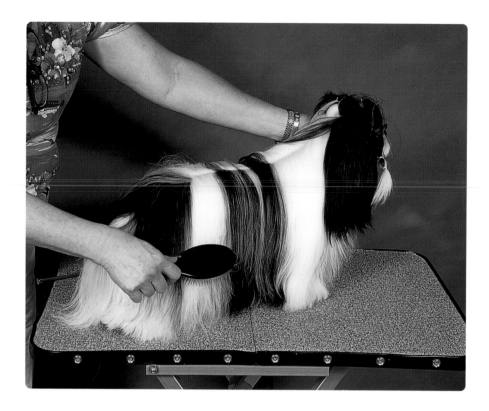

As the grooming lessons progress, you can teach your Shih Tzu to stand calmly on the table while you brush or comb her. To do this, hold her lightly with your hand between the rear legs. If she tries to move or sit down, apply gentle pressure to bring her back to the right position. Don't try to position your Shih Tzu by lifting her under the stomach or she will hunch up. Speak reassuringly in a happy voice and pet your puppy. Make these first training sessions short, no longer than five minutes.

When you are finished, give your puppy lots of praise for cooperating and set her on the floor. You might want to give her a small food reward or make a clicker sound. Whatever you do, be sure to do the same thing in the same order every time. Make it a routine. This is your way of letting your Shih Tzu know that her table time has ended and that she did a good job.

If you have the time, repeat these mini-training sessions two or three times a day until your Shih Tzu feels comfortable sitting, lying, and standing on the grooming table.

Advanced Grooming Training

Once your Shih Tzu is accustomed to lying or standing on the grooming table and remains still without trying to jump off the table, you can begin training her to be handled, sprayed, brushed, combed, clipped, and dried on the tabletop.

Working Around the Face and Toenails

You may begin working on and around your pet's face after she has learned to accept having her body brushed and combed. Make sure your Shih Tzu is well-trained before you work with scissors or other objects near her eyes and ears.

Start by scratching the ears and under the chin. Take a soft cotton cloth or tissue and gently wipe the corners of the eyes, the muzzle, and then the corners of the nostrils. Lift the lips and open the mouth. Try to perform these activities in the same order. Make them a brief, but repetitive, routine followed by plenty of praise. Continue to handle and lift the feet. If all is proceeding well, now is a good time to pretend to use the nail clippers. Let your companion become familiar with the sound the clippers make, set them on the nails, but do not cut the nails.

It will take several sessions before your Shih Tzu has completely adapted to the routine of lying or standing on the grooming table and being handled, brushed, and combed.

To avoid startling and possibly injuring your puppy, introduce her to spray bottles, electric clippers, and hair dryers and the sounds they make while she is on the ground. After your Shih Tzu is used to these items, you can use them while she stands on the grooming table.

When your puppy is used to the sound of electric clippers, place her on the grooming table and turn on the clippers. Do not clip the coat. Remove the blades and practice setting and moving the clippers against your puppy's body so that she can become familiar with the sensation.

Several lessons later, you can train your Shih Tzu to stand on the table while you dry her coat with a hair dryer. Many owners prefer to towel dry their Shih Tzu, but a hair dryer can speed up the job and produce beautiful results. While drying the coat you can also inspect the skin, as the dryer separates the hairs. Begin by simply turning the dryer on a low setting and holding it away from your pet. If she is startled and wants to run away, pet her and talk to her calmly until she relaxes. Do not use the dryer on the coat yet. At each grooming session to follow, turn on the dryer and hold it away from your dog. When your Shih Tzu is no longer bothered by the sound of the dryer (this may take several sessions), you can begin by lightly spraying water on the coat and then gently blowing air on her back with the dryer on a low setting. Eventually, your Shih Tzu will get used to the hair dryer and you may use it on the sides, shoulders, and neck.

Leash Training

1 Place a soft collar around your puppy's neck. Although she will scratch a bit, in no time at all she will forget it is even there. Attach a leash to the collar and let your puppy just pull it around for a few short periods.

2 Pick up the leash and follow your puppy around wherever she wants to go.

3 Hold a little treat in your fingers and begin to coax the puppy to follow you. Stay a few steps ahead of her and encourage her to come to you for the treat. Never pull or jerk on the leash.

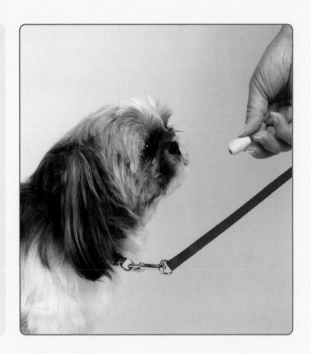

4 Within a day or two your puppy will begin to follow along with you. If she suddenly sits down or balks, use the treat to entice her.

The *Sit* Command

1 Place your puppy in front of you, facing you. Let her smell the small treat in your hand but hold on to it and don't let her have it. Keep the treat in your hand. Raise your hand above your puppy's head. As her nose follows the treat, she must lower her rump and drop into a sitting position. Keep your hand lightly on her nose so she does not jump up.

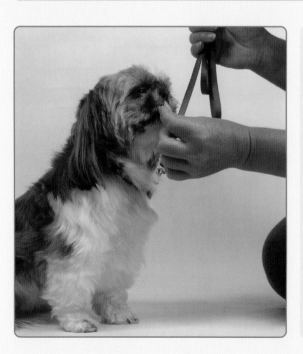

2 The moment your puppy is in a sitting position, say "Yes!" (or click) and give her the treat and praise her. When you are ready to release your puppy, give her a release signal, such as "okay" or a double-click.

3 When your puppy has learned this action, introduce the word "sit." In the beginning, your puppy will not understand that she is to remain in the *sit* position until you give the release signal. If she tries to stand up or leave before you give the release signal, place your hand gently on her back to teach her to wait in the *sit* position. When you give the release signal, remove your hand from her back. In a few lessons, placing your hand on your puppy's back will not be necessary.

4 You may alternate hands for this exercise and as your puppy learns the skill, you can take your hand off her nose and eventually use your hand to signal the command. Your puppy will soon associate *sit* with the word, action, and hand signal. Always pet and praise your puppy after her lesson.

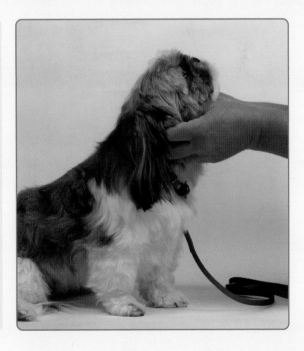

The *Stay* Command

1 Make your Shih Tzu stay in the sit position for increasing lengths of time. Begin with a few seconds and increase the time as lessons progress over the following weeks. Don't test a very young puppy's patience to the limits. As bright as the Shih Tzu is as a breed, remember you are dealing with a baby. The attention span of any puppy is relatively short.

2 With your Shih Tzu on a leash and sitting in front of you, give her the *sit* command.

3 Put the palm of your right hand in front of her eyes and say "Stay!" Any attempt on her part to get up must be corrected at once, returning her to the *sit* position, holding your palm up, and repeating "Stay!"

4 Once she begins to understand what you want, you can gradually increase the distance by stepping back. With a long leash attached to her collar (lightweight lead is fine) start with a few steps and gradually increase the distance to several yards.

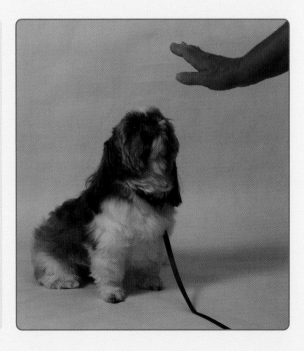

Activities

Shih Tzu are smart, talented, dynamic, nimble, quick, and fun loving—the perfect combination for a top competitor in the show ring, agility ring, and beyond! Shih Tzu put their hearts into anything fun that puts them at the center of attention. Here are some ways you can put your Shih Tzu's talents to the test.

Dog Shows

Dog shows are a lot of fun for both exhibitors and observers. Dogs are judged on how closely they come to the ideal standard for conformation for their breeds. If your Shih Tzu is gorgeous enough to compete against the best of her breed, consider joining a Shih Tzu club, as well as a local kennel club. These clubs can provide you with information on show dates and locations, judges, professional handlers, canine activities, and even offer handling classes to teach you and your dog the ropes. Dog clubs also organize fun matches—dog shows where you can practice and perfect what you've learned before you participate in an all-breed or specialty show. Fun Matches are hosted by American Kennel Club (AKC) approved breed clubs and are conducted according to AKC show rules. Only purebred, AKC registered dogs may participate. Fun matches do not count toward points for a championship and dogs that have won points toward a championship do not compete. Judges at fun matches may be official AKC judges, or knowledgeable dog breeders or handlers selected by the hosting club.

Specialty Shows

Under the AKC show regulations, there are two types of conformation shows. They are specialty and group shows, and all-breed shows. Dogs are judged according to their breed standard and, by a process of elimination, one dog is selected as Best of Breed.

A specialty show is limited to a designated breed or grouping of breeds. For example, the Shih Tzu Club of America holds an annual show for Shih Tzu only. The show is held under AKC rules and held by the individual breed clubs.

The Shih Tzu Club of America is responsible for maintaining the official standards of the breed. If there are any changes or revisions to be made, the club must approve them before submitting them for final approval to the AKC.

To become a champion, your Shih Tzu must win a minimum of 15 points by competing in formal American Kennel Club–sanctioned, licensed events. The points must be accumulated as major wins under different judges.

Breed Truths

Therapy Dog Extraordinaire

Nothing brightens the day more than a smile—especially a Shih Tzu grin! Shih Tzu make wonderful pet-facilitated therapy dogs for adult day-care centers and health-care facilities. A well-mannered, well-trained, gorgeously groomed, little lion dog can play a big role bringing happiness and affection to the lives of many patients. Shih Tzu fit any lap and every heart!

All-Breed Shows

As the name implies, all-breed shows are for all different breeds. Judging is conducted according to AKC rules. In addition to Best of Breed winners, open shows offer the titles of Best in Group (for dogs considered to be the best representative of their group) and Best in Show (for the dog selected as the best representative of its breed and group, compared to dogs of other breeds and groups).

Obedience Trials

Shih Tzu can be tough competitors in obedience. Your little "lion dog" is smart, and in obedience competitions it's intelligence that counts—both canine and human! Your dog must be smart enough to learn the commands, and *you* must be clever enough to find a training method that works.

In obedience trials, dogs are put through a series of exercises and commands and judged according to performance. Each dog starts out with 200 points. Points are subtracted throughout the trials for lack of attention, nonperformance, barking, or slowness.

Obedience trials are divided into three levels, each progressive level is more difficult and challenging: Novice—Companion Dog (C.D.), Open—Companion Dog Excellent (C.D.X.), and Utility—Utility Dog (U.D.) and Utility Dog Excellent (U.D.X.).

What does it take to earn a U.D.X., the toughest and most coveted of all obedience titles? The dog and her trainer/handler must pass the Open and Utility classes on the same day. Could a Shih Tzu accomplish such a feat? Absolutely! In 1998 a Shih Tzu earned the U.D.X. for the first time in the history of the breed.

Agility Competitions

Agility competitions are exciting, fast-paced, timed events in which dogs complete challenging obstacle courses, jump over objects, teeter on seesaws, walk planks, run through tunnels, jump through hoops, and weave in and out between poles. Titles that your Shih Tzu can earn, in increasing level of difficulty, are: Novice Agility (NA), Open Agility (OA), Agility Excellent (AX), and Master Agility Excellent (MX).

Preparation for the agility course includes advanced training sessions and lots of strengthening and conditioning exercises. After all, as an agility dog, your little toy is an athlete in the truest sense of the word.

Canine Good Citizen

Your Shih Tzu can earn a Canine Good Citizen award from the American Kennel Club just by proving she has good manners and knows her stuff. The program consists of a series of ten tests that allow your Shih Tzu to prove that she knows how to behave properly at home, in the community, and around other dogs. The ten tests are

1. Accepting a friendly stranger
2. Sitting politely for petting
3. Appearance and grooming
4. Out for a walk (on a loose lead)
5. Walking through a crowd
6. *Sit* and *down* on command and *stay* in place
7. Coming when called
8. Reaction to another dog
9. Reaction to distraction
10. Supervised separation

For more information on the Canine Good Citizen award, as well as any of the activities listed above, visit the American Kennel Club Web site at *www.akc.org*.

Therapy Work

Shih Tzu are wonderful companions. They form strong bonds with their owners, are very protective of them, and make excellent watchdogs. Shih Tzu are also talented service and therapy dogs. Whether saving or simply enriching lives, busy Shih Tzu work their magic in countless ways every day.

Shih Tzu Hearing Dogs

Shih Tzu make excellent hearing dogs and can serve as ears for their hearing-impaired owners. Shih Tzu can learn to run to the source of the sound (such as a fire alarm, doorbell, knock, voice, smoke alarm, or telephone), back to their owners, and back again to the sound. In this way Shih Tzu alert their owners to possible dangers and make it possible for people to be more independent and feel more secure.

Chapter Eight

Shih Tzu Grooming

Grooming is an essential part of your Shih Tzu's health care program. The stunning, profuse, flowing coat for which the Shih Tzu is recognized is not created overnight. It takes daily grooming, nutritious food, excellent health care, and the right genetics for a Shih Tzu to grow a long, gorgeous coat.

Your Shih Tzu must be combed, brushed, and bathed routinely to keep her coat healthy, shiny, and free of mats. Severely matted hair cannot be untangled; you will have to cut the mats out with scissors, and this will make your little companion look uneven and ragged. But grooming is not just for cosmetic purposes. If the coat becomes matted, its insulating quality will be lost. Mats are also good hiding places for parasites, such as fleas, ticks, and mites.

Grooming is fun! You and your Shih Tzu will enjoy each other's company and strengthen the human-animal bond you share. It will take lots of practice (and maybe some helpful tips from accomplished Shih Tzu groomers), but in time you will develop your own favorite grooming techniques that keep your Shih Tzu looking "show ring ready." (To learn more on how to prepare your pet for grooming, see Chapter Seven, "Grooming Training," page 110.)

Here are some tips to make grooming sessions fun and enjoyable.

- Set up a regular grooming schedule.
- Choose a time and day when you have plenty of time to get the job done without being rushed or stressed.
- Gather your materials and supplies and place them within convenient reach of your work area and the grooming table.
- Train your Shih Tzu to be well mannered during grooming sessions and to sit and stand on the grooming table (see Chapter Seven, "Table Training," page 111).

Fun Facts

People can lower their blood pressure simply by touching or caressing an animal. Many Shih Tzu owners groom their dogs for relaxation and for artistic expression.

Brushing and Bathing

You should bathe your Shih Tzu at least once every three to four weeks. Spray your Shih Tzu lightly with water and a small amount of gentle hair rinse designed for canines. Gently and thoroughly brush through the coat. Make sure the hair is always moist; dry hair will break. Separate the hair down to the skin, using a comb or knitting needle to part the hair. Remove knots and tangles. Remove large mats with scissors. Pay special attention to the axillary (armpit) regions, groin areas (inside of thighs), belly, behind and under the ears, and below the anus. These areas tend to become matted or soiled and are often overlooked. Remove mats from these areas.

Helpful Hints

Always brush your Shih Tzu well *before* you give her a bath. If you don't remove knots, tangles, and mats before you bathe your pet, they will become fixed in the coat when it gets wet and they will be even more difficult to remove later.

Express (empty) the anal sacs *before* you bathe your Shih Tzu. Anal sacs are located at either side of the inside of the rectum. If the sacs are not expressed, or emptied, on a regular basis, they can become impacted, infected, or abscessed and rupture. To empty anal sacs, wear disposable gloves. Place an absorbent tissue over the anus to absorb sac contents. Anal sac contents are normally brown in color and have a foul odor. Find the sacs through the perianal tissue by lightly pressing on each side of the anus. The anal sacs feel like small grapes. Gently squeeze on the sacs from the outside of the anus, with your thumb and index finger, until they empty into the tissue.

To bathe your Shih Tzu, first place a hair trap over the drain. Place a non-slip mat in the bottom of the sink or tub. Set the water to a comfortable temperature. Put a large, soft cotton ball in your Shih Tzu's ear canals to prevent water entry. Thoroughly wet the coat. Mix some emollient shampoo with warm water and apply it to the coat. Wash the coat and rinse it thoroughly. Pour a mixture of crème rinse and warm water over the coat and work it in well. Rinse again, leaving in just enough of the rinse that the coat feels barely slick (not sticky or gooey) and gently squeeze as much water as possible out of the coat.

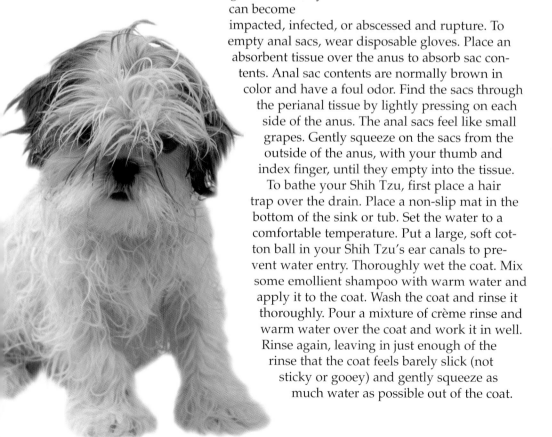

CHECKLIST

Grooming Supplies

- ✔ grooming table
- ✔ non-slip mat and towels
- ✔ soft brush
- ✔ brush with flexible pins
- ✔ fine slicker brush
- ✔ comb with rotating pins
- ✔ comb that is fine on one end and coarse on the other (teeth spacing)
- ✔ parting comb
- ✔ rake comb
- ✔ scissors (blunt-tipped)
- ✔ eye ointment to protect eyes during bath
- ✔ nail trimmers
- ✔ spray bottle
- ✔ bows and elastic bands
- ✔ hair gel, hairspray
- ✔ cornstarch
- ✔ emollient shampoo (pH balanced for dog skin)
- ✔ gentle hair rinse (developed for dogs)
- ✔ self-rinse shampoo
- ✔ ear cleaning solution (available from your veterinarian)
- ✔ cotton-tipped swabs, cotton balls
- ✔ washcloth
- ✔ paper towels
- ✔ hair dryer
- ✔ electric hair clippers
- ✔ extra clipper blades (#4, #5, #7, #10, #15)
- ✔ electric nail sander (optional)

To dry the coat, first blot excess water from the coat with a towel. Dry your Shih Tzu thoroughly. Dry the ears well with a soft, dry cloth. Use a cotton-tipped swab to dry and clean the ear canals, but do not probe too deeply or you could rupture the eardrum. Make sure the ears are dry. Germs grow rapidly in moist ears and Shih Tzu are prone to ear infections.

Blow-dry the hair with a hair dryer by separating the hair in strands or layers as you dry it. Make sure the hair dryer is not hot and does not dry or burn your Shih Tzu's skin.

Helpful Hints

If you cannot do the detail grooming, take your Shih Tzu to a professional groomer on a regular basis (a *minimum* of once every three weeks is recommended) or consider having her body clipped. The clipped look doesn't have the aesthetic impact of a spectacular, long, flowing coat, but it is practical, easier to comb and keep clean, and cooler in the summer.

Clipping Nails

Shih Tzu need to have their toenails clipped regularly, especially because they spend most of their time indoors, so they don't wear down their nails on hard surfaces. Check your Shih Tzu's nails often and don't let them become overgrown. Trim them at least once a month or ask your veterinarian or groomer to trim them. Overgrown nails can deform the paws, interfere with

movement, and hinder your Shih Tzu's ability to walk. In more severe cases, they can curve under and pierce the footpads.

To determine if your Shih Tzu needs a nail trim, stand her on the grooming table. None of the nails should touch the surface of the table. Notice that each toenail curves and tapers into a point. If the toenail is not too dark in color, you will be able to see pink inside of the toenail, or the "quick." This is the blood supply; just below the blood supply is the excess nail growth needed to be removed. If the toenails are too dark to differentiate where the quick ends, you can illuminate the nail with a penlight or a flashlight to find the line of demarcation where the blood supply ends.

There are different types of nail trimmers. Most Shih Tzu owners prefer the guillotine-style clippers. To use these you place the toenail inside the metal loop, align the upper and lower blades with the area to cut, and squeeze the clipper handles. Cut only the very tip of the toenail. If the nail is still too long, continue to carefully remove the end of the nail in small increments. If you accidentally cut too close, stop the bleeding by applying styptic powder (a clotting powder commercially available from your pet store or veterinarian) or styptic sticks (human shaving sticks). You can also stop the bleeding by applying pressure to the nail with a clean cloth for five minutes. Invest in a pet electric nail filer to smooth nail tips.

Breed Truths

Bad breath in dogs is a sign of possible health problems, including

- periodontal disease
- foreign body obstructing nasal passages
- infection or ulcers (tonsils, lips, gums, cheeks, tongue)
- metabolic diseases

Dental Care

Dental care is one of the most important aspects of your Shih Tzu's health care program and should start while your Shih Tzu is still a puppy.

Puppies are born without teeth. When Shih Tzu reach three to four weeks of age, their deciduous teeth (baby teeth) start to erupt. At around 4 months, these 28 temporary teeth begin to fall out and are replaced with 48 permanent teeth. During this time, Shih Tzu puppies want to chew on everything and should be given lots of safe chew toys. By six months of age, all of the adult teeth should be in place. These teeth must last a lifetime, so it is important to take good care of them by preventing plaque and tartar buildup and periodontal disease.

Plaque buildup can be reduced by dental brushing. Brushing baby teeth is good for practice and training. If you practice on your Shih Tzu puppy, she will be quite used to the routine by the time her adult teeth have erupted.

Purchase a soft-bristle toothbrush and dog toothpaste recommended by your veterinarian or local pet supply store. Do not use human toothpaste. Many human products contain spearmint or peppermint or other substances that cause dogs to salivate (drool) profusely or upset their stomachs.

Start with the upper front teeth (incisors), brushing down and away from the gum line, or in a gentle, circular motion. Proceed back to the premolars and molars on one side of the mouth. Repeat on the upper teeth on the opposite side of the mouth. When you brush the bottom teeth, pay particular attention to the incisors.

Shih Tzu can be somewhat undershot. This means that the lower jaw (mandible) protrudes or extends in front of the upper jaw (maxilla). Shih Tzu may have a missing tooth or slightly misaligned teeth. Keep this in mind as you look for possible problem areas as you brush your Shih Tzu's teeth.

From the incisors, work back to the molars, brushing up and away from the gum line. Repeat on the lower teeth on the opposite side of the mouth.

In the beginning, keep dental brushing sessions short so your puppy will tolerate them better. Spend about one minute on the upper teeth and then praise your puppy for good behavior. Later in the day you can spend another one-minute time increment on the bottom teeth.

Breed Needs

Regular dental brushing is important, but it is not a replacement for veterinary dental visits. Even with the best of care, most Shih Tzu require routine professional dental cleaning and polishing.

Grooming Tips

Gently and carefully wipe debris away from your Shih Tzu's eyes with a soft, clean, damp washcloth. Wipe from the inner corner of the eye downward and outward. If your Shih Tzu's eyes frequently tear, the hair will be stained a red brown color at the inner corners of the eyes. Prolonged tearing is a sign of eye problems. Consult your veterinarian about the cause of your Shih Tzu's tearing and how to treat it before the problem becomes serious. Your veterinarian can also provide you with a product, safe for use around the eyes, to help eliminate the stain.

Comb the hair gently away from your Shih Tzu's eyes *every day*. Loose hairs come in contact with the eyes and stick to the surface. Continual irritation from hairs can cause serious, painful conditions, such as dry eyes, infections, corneal ulcers, and blindness. Let your pet's hair grow between the eyes and at the base of the muzzle (the bridge of the nose) until it is long enough to tie up in a topknot. Do not trim these hairs unless absolutely necessary because they will require constant trimming to keep short or they will stick into the eyes and injure them. *To avoid accident or injury, use only blunt-tipped scissors and cover the eyes with your hand when you trim stray hairs away from the face and eyes.* Rinse your Shih Tzu's eyes daily with a gentle eyewash recommended by your veterinarian. Do not use eye products prescribed for yourself or for your other pets. Do not use products in the eyes that contain corticosteroids unless your veterinarian has specifically prescribed them for your Shih Tzu. *If your Shih Tzu is squinting, has reddened scleras (the normally white parts of the eyes), pale blue areas on the surface of either or both eyes, is tearing, or has a discharge from the eyes, contact your veterinarian immediately.* Clean around the muzzle, particularly at the bridge of the nose and where it comes in contact with the face between the eyes. Shih Tzu have a tendency to develop moist areas

CAUTION

When a dog is submerged in water, fleas scramble to higher ground—in this case, the dog's head. So, if your Shih Tzu has fleas, start by washing her head first and then work down her body. This helps prevent fleas from gathering around your Shih Tzu's eyes, ears, and muzzle. Suds and rinse the fleas down the body and down the drain.

at the base of the muzzle and these areas can develop bacterial or fungal infections.

Trim excess hair from the ear canals by pulling or plucking them. Clean the inside of the ears with a soft, damp cloth and dry the ears thoroughly. Do not use ear-cleaning products that contain alcohol unless your veterinarian has recommended them. Alcohol is very drying and is painful on raw, tender, or inflamed areas. If you see any discharge from the ear or smell any foul odors, contact your veterinarian immediately. Ear problems are very painful and can lead to hearing loss and problems with balance.

Trim excess hair from between the footpads with blunt-tipped scissors and trim around the feet level with the grooming table to give them a rounded appearance. Neat, trimmed feet prevent mats, dirt, foreign objects (such as grass awns), and excess moisture (leading to bacterial growth, moist dermatitis, and sores) from accumulating between the toes.

Trim excess hair away from the groin area and under the tail with blunt-tipped scissors or a #10 or #15 clipper blade.

Trim the toenails. Dewclaws (vestigial digits located where a "thumb" would be) are usually removed, but if your Shih Tzu has her dewclaws, trim those nails as well. Untrimmed dewclaws can snag and tear, or grow into footpads and tissues, causing pain and lameness.

CAUTION

Shih Tzu fit easily inside most sinks or bathtubs. If you use a sink, make sure the faucets are out of the way, so your pet doesn't bump them. Set the water to a comfortable temperature *before* you put your Shih Tzu in the sink or use the sprayer to rinse her.

Grooming Styles

There are lots of ways to groom a Shih Tzu. The "casual look" is ideal for the Shih Tzu that stays at home and goes on family outings. The "show look" requires a great deal of time and grooming skill. A short haircut or body clip is great for the practical-minded owner who only has time for a low-maintenance coat.

Topknots and Trims

The type of topknot and trim you select for your Shih Tzu will depend on how long her hair is, how much time you have to spend on grooming, convenience, and practicality. It also matters what your dog will be doing. Will she be lounging in the living room or will she be on the show circuit? If you plan to exhibit your Shih Tzu, plan on a great deal of work and grooming to maintain the coat in luxurious condition.

There are several types of topknots, body trims, leg trims, and tail trims for Shih Tzu. Certain styles of leg trims go best with particular types of body trims. With practice and experience, you will discover which topknots, trims, and cuts show off your pet's qualities and hide her minor flaws, producing the balanced, classic look of the regal Shih Tzu.

Puppies

Puppies look cutest if their hair is cut to emphasize their rounded heads. Most puppies won't have hair long enough for a topknot until they are 5 or 6 months of age. Cut the topknot with scissors so that all the hairs are about 2 inches long. Leave the beard and moustache to grow longer, up to 6 inches. Trim the ears to blend in with the facial hair to accentuate the round head.

The topknot styles you create for your Shih Tzu are limited only by your imagination. You can trim the topknot to various lengths or you can let it grow long. You can part the topknot and secure it to the ears with elastics, plastics, or bows. It's fun to select bows that go well with your pet's coat color.

To make the topknot stand up higher, comb it straight back, tease it gently, section it, band it, and curl it with a curling iron (as is done for the show ring). Curling and teasing, plus a dab of hair gel, give the topknot more support to help it stand up higher on the head so that the neck looks longer and graceful.

Kennel Cut

Shave all of the hair except for over the forehead. Cut the forehead hair and trim the ears with scissors to create a rounded skull appearance. Blend the ears in well with the sides of the head. Keep the hair out of the eyes but do not trim the base of the muzzle. For a different variation of this cut, allow the hair to grow all over the top of the head and keep it trimmed with scissors to a length of 1 to 2 inches to form a full topknot. Comb and trim the ears and beard to emphasize a rounded appearance.

Body Trims

Puppy Trim For the Shih Tzu puppy that has a thick coat and enjoys playing outdoors and getting dirty but still wants to look cute, this might be the style to choose. It is cool in summer and warm enough in winter. Trim the hair on the head 1 to 2 inches all over and trim the ears to blend in with the head. Shape the head to emphasize its rounded appearance. Leave the beard 3 to 6 inches long. The puppy trim lets your puppy keep a full tail along with a cut that emphasizes a pretty body and cylindrical legs, all in a hair length ranging from 1 to 3 inches.

Kennel Clip This is the easiest haircut to maintain because most of the hair has been removed. Clip all of the body (with a #4, #5, or #7 clipper blade) except for the end of the tail, which ends in a tuft. Leave a tuft of hair over the skull to emphasize the head's rounded appearance. Trim the feet and ears. This is a great haircut for the summertime and an ideal haircut for owners who have little time or desire to groom their Shih Tzu.

Body Clip Clip the body with a #4, #5, #7, #10, or #15 blade. Trim the hair short on the back and trim the legs 1 to 2 inches in length. Shape and bell the legs to flare out at the feet. Trim the tail at the base and leave it intact for the length of its curvature. Trim the head to accentuate a rounded look, keep the beard, and trim the ears to a bell shape to complement the leg trim. This is another great summer style with easy maintenance.

Schnauzer Style Using a #5, #7, #10, or #15 blade, trim from the skull down the neck and to the chest and body, with the trim going in the direction of the hair growth. The clipper trim stops at the bottom of the rib cage and the bottom one-third of the legs. The hairs from these areas are trimmed with scissors to a cylindrical shape and left 1 to 2 inches long. Keep the beard, and trim the ears lightly to offset a short topknot. Leave the tail in a tassel.

Cocker Cut The Cocker cut lets your Shih Tzu keep more of her hair than most cuts and gives a sense of overall balance. Clip the body with a #5, #7, #10, or #15 blade, from the top of the back of the neck to the base of the tail. If you imagine a parting down the center of your Shih Tzu's back and perpendicular to the parting about one third of the way down the side of the body (to the top of the fore limb), that's where the clipping ends. From that point on, trim the chest hairs and hairs on the sides of the body and the leg hairs about 4 to 5 inches in length. Taper the legs down to the feet, round the ears, and flag the tail.

Full-Furnishings Clip Furnishings refer to all the long hair responsible for embellishing and accentuating the look for which the Shih Tzu breed is recognized and famous. Furnishings include the beard and topknot and long hairs on the ears, limbs (also called skirts or pants on the hindquarters), belly, face, and tail.

In the full-furnishings clip, only the neck and back are clipped (in a Cocker-style clip), while the legs, sides of the body, and tail are left full length or trimmed level with the grooming table.

This style is difficult to maintain and requires the most time and work. When properly maintained, it is also the most aesthetically appealing and impressive style.

The time and effort you invest in your Shih Tzu's coat and skin will keep her looking beautiful and in top condition. As you become more familiar with the Shih Tzu standard and develop more skill at grooming, you will find ways to groom your dog so that you can enhance her features to more closely reflect the ideal Shih Tzu. The more you practice, the more skilled you will become, and the better your little "lion dog" will look. Even if your Shih Tzu isn't competing in the show ring, she will always be *Best in Show* at your home!

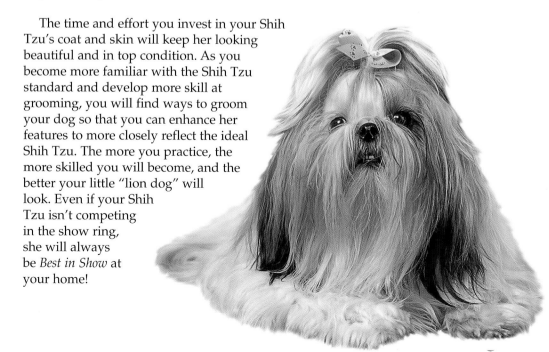

Chapter Nine

The Senior Shih Tzu

S hih Tzu live longer than most breeds. In fact, with excellent care, that Shih Tzu puppy you have just fallen in love with could possibly live fifteen years or more, perhaps into her late teens or even early twenties. On the Shih Tzu life span timeline, the puppy stage is relatively short, about 12 to 18 months; the adolescent and mature adult is an additional six to seven years; and beyond that, the majority of adult years are senior years. In other words, more than half, perhaps two-thirds, of your Shih Tzu's life will be spent as a senior.

Just as puppies require special care, so do older dogs. Some Shih Tzu age more slowly and have fewer health problems than others. This is especially true for Shih Tzu that receive lots of love and attention, good health care, and quality nutrition throughout their lives.

Neither you, nor your veterinarian, can *prevent* the normal aging process, but there are some things you both can do to *slow* the progression of health problems caused by aging. You can do a lot to enrich your Shih Tzu's quality of life so that she ages gracefully and comfortably in her golden years.

Age-Related Changes

As Shih Tzu age, they seem unaware of the gradual restrictions and limitations aging puts on their bodies. They can no longer run and play as enthusiastically as they did when they were youngsters, but they might try. When geriatric Shih Tzu overexert, injury can result. For example, aging usually causes some degree of arthritis (painful joints) and muscle weakness and atrophy (shrinkage). As a result, movement becomes painful, limited, and stiff. Things that were once easy to do are now dangerous, such as jumping on and off furniture. Geriatric Shih Tzu enjoy leisurely strolls on soft surfaces but they should not be forced to go on extended,

Breed Truths

A Shih Tzu is considered a senior when she reaches seven years of age.

FYI: Signs of Aging

Signs of Aging	Problems
Gray, white, or silver hairs where they did not grow before, especially along the sides of the face, eyebrows, muzzle	None
Less supple skin, body odor, thin coat, warts, moles, cysts, lumps, and growths on skin	Odor may indicate health problem, growths may be cancerous
Tires easily, takes long, frequent naps	Aging heart, congestive heart failure, other organ problems
Changes in sleeping and waking cycles	May stay up during the night, pacing, or whining and then may sleep throughout the day
Changes in social interactions	Less interest in life, plays less, withdraws from owner, family, and other animals. Can become extremely withdrawn and, in rare instances, even aggressive
Arthritis	Joint pain, joint trauma, muscle weakness, stiff or painful movement and gait, moves at a slower pace than in previous years
Slow metabolic rate	Metabolic rates slow with aging, leading to weight gain and obesity in some individuals. Obesity can lead to joint pain, diabetes, heart disease, and other health problems
Bad breath, plaque and tartar accumulation on teeth, worn teeth, swollen gums, periodontal disease	Dental disease can lead to systemic bacterial infections and abscesses in the heart, liver, kidney, and other organs
Cataracts	Some cataracts are caused by aging, some are caused by diabetes. Certain kinds of cataracts can be surgically removed.
Deafness	Dogs lose hearing ability as they age. As hearing fails and eyesight worsens, Shih Tzu rely more on senses of smell and touch.
Urinary incontinence	Many dogs lose some degree of urinary bladder control as they age. Urinary incontinence varies from dribbling to complete lack of bladder control. The condition is more common in geriatric, spayed females, than in males.

What You Can Do

Nothing

Provide good nutrition for skin and coat care, bathe regularly in gentle shampoo and rinse, have veterinarian check growths

Medications are available by prescription, if needed. Rest, avoid stress and excessive exercise

Spend time with your Shih Tzu during the day to help her sleep more at night. Consult your veterinarian.

Although this profound change in behavior is stressful, do not force interaction when your Shih Tzu wants to be left alone. Consult your veterinarian.

Prevent jumping; avoid stairs, hills, hard surfaces, excessive or strenuous exercise; carry your Shih Tzu when she is tired. Veterinary exam, x-rays, medicine for pain and inflammation, if needed.

Feed correct diet for age and activity level, do not overfeed. Your Shih Tzu may benefit from a prescription diet.

Veterinary dental cleaning, tooth extractions, and antibiotics to prevent spread of infection throughout body

Approach your Shih Tzu slowly while speaking to her so you do not startle her if she does not see you. Ask your veterinarian to refer you to a veterinary ophthalmologist to learn if your Shih Tzu is a good candidate for cataract surgery.

Approach your Shih Tzu from the front so she sees you. Speak kindly, but loudly to get her attention.

Consult your veterinarian to be sure the problem is limited to bladder control and is not due to serious kidney, bladder, or neurological problems. Medications are available to help treat the condition.

FYI: Signs of Aging

Signs of Aging	Problems
Bowel problems	Bowel problems and lack of bowel control have many causes, including food allergies, food intolerance, malabsorption, parasites, diseases, neurological problems, and tumors of the gastrointestinal tract.
Decreased immunity and lowered disease resistance	Deterioration of the immune system, immune suppression, auto-immune diseases, cancer, and tumor formation
Disorientation (senility) and cognitive dysfunction	Multiple causes, including normal aging, toxicity due to organ failure, brain tumor. Animal may seem to "forget" to eliminate in the appropriate places and is confused.
Overall deterioration in health condition, weight loss	Heart, liver, kidney, pancreas, lungs, and other organ failure; cancer; hormonal imbalances; stress; multiple causes

CAUTION

Shih Tzu love to be as high up and as close to "eye level" with their owners as possible. They were bred to be carried, cuddled, and coddled. So it is natural that they do not like to be down low on the ground for long periods of time. When you are not present, or are unable, to safely lift and carry your Shih Tzu, you can still help prevent injury by buying or building a safe, non-slip ramp for your Shih Tzu to walk up to and down from her favorite areas "on high"—such as the sofa or bed. Ramps are also helpful to replace short flights of stairs and help prevent trauma to your pet's joints. Just be sure the ramp is large enough so that your Shih Tzu cannot fall off of it.

rigorous walks. Shih Tzu should not be exercised on hard surfaces. Excessive exercise can be harmful to an aging Shih Tzu.

As a Shih Tzu ages, her body's metabolic rate slows. This can lead to weight gain, a weaker heart, a reduction in organ function (especially liver and kidneys), muscle weakening and shrinkage, and a gradual overall deterioration in the dog's health and condition. This decline in health is often accompanied by a decreased resistance to diseases, or immune suppression, and can be caused or worsened by stress.

If a normally mild-mannered Shih Tzu is suddenly irritated by other animals or people, or seeks isolation from the family, or seems disoriented, these are signs of a serious problem.

What You Can Do

Consult your veterinarian

Give your Shih Tzu attention that will cause her to relax, such as a gentle massage or enjoyable grooming session. Consult your veterinarian.

Provide cognitive stimulation, such as asking your Shih Tzu to sit or down or shake and then reward her with a new and interesting toy. Medication is available to treat dogs with some types of cognitive dysfunction.

Consult veterinarian

The Shih Tzu may be very sick or in pain. Strange behavioral changes can also indicate a stroke or cognitive dysfunction (senility).

Age-related changes, and the rate at which they occur, vary between Shih Tzu. Aging is influenced by many factors, including health, genetics, nutrition, environment, hormones, and the type of care received throughout life. You may not have control over all of these factors, but if you act quickly and contact your veterinarian, together you may be able to slow down the progression of your Shih Tzu's health problems.

Helpful Hints

Older Shih Tzu are more sensitive and less adaptable to hot and cold temperatures. Keep your Shih Tzu housed at a comfortable temperature (room temperature) so that she does not get too cold or overheat.

Dental Disease

Periodontal disease can harm more than your Shih Tzu's teeth and gums. The bacteria that live in the mouth and proliferate along the gums and teeth can gain entry into the bloodstream through diseased gums. From there bacteria travel in the blood throughout the body and lodge and multiply in various body organs, such as heart

valves, liver, kidney, and spleen, where they form abscesses, or eventually cause death. If your Shih Tzu has dental problems, consult your veterinarian immediately!

Reduce Stress

As your Shih Tzu ages, she will become more sensitive to stress. One of the most stressful things for many senior Shih Tzu is leaving home, even for a short period. Your Shih Tzu may have loved traveling everywhere with you before, but do not be surprised if she now prefers to stay at home. Travel can be very stressful to old dogs. If your Shih Tzu has become a homebody in her golden years, leave her at home.

A highly stressful situation for most senior Shih Tzu is being housed in a boarding facility. Whether the boarding takes place at a commercial kennel facility or a veterinary hospital, these environments are seldom the "home away from home" they claim to be. They are often noisy, stressful, uncomfortable, and a likely place to contract contagious (infectious) diseases, especially respiratory and intestinal diseases. Even though your Shih Tzu is up-to-date on her vaccinations, like many geriatric dogs, she may have a suppressed

CAUTION

Contact your veterinarian immediately if your Shih Tzu shows any signs of behavioral change, if she refuses to eat or drink, or if she appears to be in pain or discomfort.

CHECKLIST

Keeping Your Shih Tzu Comfortable in Her Golden Years

✔ Keep your Shih Tzu warm and dry. Senior Shih Tzu do not tolerate cold temperatures well. Arthritis is more painful in cold weather.

✔ Give your Shih Tzu a soft, warm, bed made of natural products (cotton, wool).

✔ Make sure your Shih Tzu has a *non-slip*, soft surface on which to rise, stand, and walk. Hard surfaces are painful on old joints.

✔ Weigh your Shih Tzu once every month to be sure she is not overweight or underweight. Overweight or obese dogs have more health problems and joint pain. Sudden weight change, especially weight loss, is a sign of a health problem.

✔ Take your Shih Tzu out several times a day for short, easy, leisurely strolls on level, soft, non-slippery surfaces. Walk on grass or sand when possible. Avoid hills, steep slopes, and stairs.

✔ When you take your Shih Tzu for walks, let her set the pace. Do not walk too far or too fast. Keep her toenails trimmed.

✔ Do not allow your Shih Tzu to jump up on furniture, climb stairs, or walk on hard, slippery surfaces. Lift her and carry her when she needs to be carried. Buy or build a safe ramp for her.

✔ Feed a diet appropriate for your Shih Tzu's age and health condition. Feed small, frequent, nutritious meals, according to your Shih Tzu's activity level and needs. Consult your veterinarian about the best diet for your Shih Tzu, including possible benefits of a prescription diet.

✔ If your Shih Tzu has dental problems, take care of them. Make sure her food is small and soft enough to eat.

✔ If your Shih Tzu has gastrointestinal problems or food allergies, feed her a bland diet, or a prescription diet, recommended by your veterinarian.

✔ Senior Shih Tzu have a high dietary protein requirement. Studies have shown that an increase in protein quality and quantity can be very beneficial for some geriatric dogs and may have anticancer and antidiabetes effects.

✔ Feed your Shih Tzu a quality diet appropriate for her age, health, teeth, and activity level. Ask your veterinarian about prescription diets available to treat, improve, or help prevent specific medical conditions.

✔ Take your Shih Tzu to your veterinarian at least once every six months for a complete physical examination to detect health problems early. Ask your veterinarian to help you target the ideal weight for your Shih Tzu's size, age, and stage of life. Lab work is necessary to monitor health conditions, such as diabetes, or liver and kidney problems.

✔ Dental disease is common in old Shih Tzu. Tooth extractions and dental cleaning require anesthesia. Old and overweight Shih Tzu are sensitive to anesthesia and are high-risk patients.

✔ Take your Shih Tzu out often to urinate and defecate. Senior Shih Tzu cannot control their bladder and bowels as well as young dogs.

✔ Give your Shih Tzu a gentle massage to relieve muscle pain.

immune system. The added stress of being away from you and her cozy home and placed in a boarding kennel can further reduce her immunity.

When you must go away, ask a family member or friend to pet sit or come to your home at least three times daily to check on and care for your senior Shih Tzu. This is a much better alternative than boarding your pet.

Be sure to leave the dog sitter the following information:

- a phone number where you can be reached in case of questions or emergency
- a detailed list of care and feeding instructions and any special concerns
- a list of any medications to give, the amount, and the times to give them
- your veterinarian's name, address, and phone number
- the name, address, and phone number of the nearest veterinary emergency hospital
- a signed document stating the dog sitter has your permission to act as your agent/representative to take your Shih Tzu to the veterinary hospital for care
- the name and number of an alternate contact in case of emergency: if you cannot return home as scheduled or if the dog sitter cannot take care of your Shih Tzu the entire time you are absent

CAUTION

Some Shih Tzu can have vaccine reactions, especially if she has been previously vaccinated, or if she is given several vaccines at one time. If your senior Shih Tzu has been vaccinated regularly throughout most of her life, she may only need core vaccinations at three-year or greater intervals, depending on her health and risk of disease exposure. Consult your veterinarian.

Saying Goodbye

Your Shih Tzu will play a big role in your life for many years. She might be your childhood friend and confidant, the dog that loves you from grade school through college; she can be the devoted friend that is always there for you during life's surprises: graduation, marriage, births, new jobs, personal accomplishments. She could be your best friend, the toy lap dog that keeps you company during your retirement. Or perhaps she is your personal therapy dog, watching over you protectively as you recover from an illness. In many ways, your life stages may be measured by the time you share with your Shih Tzu—in "Shih Tzu years," so to speak.

Your Shih Tzu is more than a precious pet. She is a genuine member of your family. And so, when the time comes to say goodbye to her, the grief you will feel can be just as profound as the grief you feel at the loss of a human loved one. It is no wonder that owners dread and delay discussing euthanasia with their veterinarians, even when they know it is nearing time to let go.

Euthanasia means putting an animal to death humanely and painlessly. Veterinarians euthanize dogs by giving a lethal substance by intravenous injection that ends life almost instantly and peacefully. A sedative is usually given a few minutes before the lethal injection, to relax the animal and make her sleepy.

If you are not sure about the right time to euthanize your Shih Tzu, ask your veterinarian for guidance. As a general rule, if your Shih Tzu's suffering cannot be relieved, or if she refuses to eat or drink, or if her quality of life is poor and the bad days outnumber the good, then it is time to discuss euthanasia with your veterinarian.

Your veterinarian can answer any questions you may have. If you wish, you can be present to hold and reassure your Shih Tzu during the euthanasia. Some veterinarians make euthanasia house calls so the animal does not have to travel and can pass peacefully at home. If you need information on pet cemeteries or cremation services, your veterinarian can give you the information you need.

Breed Truths

Shih Tzu are very intelligent and they never stop learning. More important, your loving toy companion will never stop trying to please you, even in her old age. Just be reasonable in your demands and expectations. Your senior Shih Tzu may take a little longer to learn because her hearing and sight are not as keen as when she was young. Her memory may not be quite as sharp, either, so she may need a gentle reminder now and then. Do not ask your Shih Tzu to do tricks that are strenuous or that could hurt her neck, back, limbs, muscles, or joints. Make learning fun and keep it interesting. When it comes to Shih Tzu, you can teach an old dog new tricks!

The fact that your Shih Tzu lived a long, full life is testament to the excellent care you gave her. She will leave you with years of wonderful memories to hold in your heart to help relieve your sorrow.

Chapter Ten

Special Considerations

Should Your Shih Tzu Be Neutered?

One of the most important health decisions you will make for your Shih Tzu is whether to have her neutered. Neutering is also referred to as a *gonadectomy*, meaning the removal of the gonads, the tissues in the body associated with reproduction: testicles in the male, ovaries and uterus in the female.

Female Shih Tzu usually come into estrus (also called "in heat" or "in season") around six months of age and cycle approximately every six months thereafter, depending on their family genetics. Male Shih Tzu are usually sexually mature (able to reproduce) by ten months of age.

Historically, and until recently, dog owners were routinely advised to have their dogs neutered early in life. One of the main reasons for this recommendation was to reduce the number of unwanted pets in animal shelters. In addition, research has shown that neutering dogs can offer several medical benefits. For example, females spayed before their first estrous cycle have a significantly reduced chance of developing mammary (breast) cancer later in life. Mammary cancer is not unusual in older dogs and is often life-threatening. An ovariohysterectomy also eliminates the chances that a female will have ovarian cancer. In males, neutering (castration) eliminates the risk of testicular and epididymal cancer and helps relieve or prevent some prostatic problems. Neutering has also been credited with reducing aggression and some behavioral problems in males.

Early neutering was formally approved by the American Veterinary Medical Association in 1993. Studies have shown that prepubertal gonadectomy, on pups under 16 weeks of age, does not affect growth rate, food intake, or the weight gain of growing dogs, although some delay in epiphyseal closure of the long bones has been documented.

Recently, additional studies have shown that, in addition to the inherent risks of anesthesia and surgery, neutering may possibly cause problems later in a dog's life. For example, it has long been known that females that have been spayed can develop some degree of urinary incontinence in their senior years (this problem can be treated with medication). There are also medical cases to indicate that neutering may not be the best choice for all animals. *The fact is, no medical or surgical procedure is ever completely without risk or possible side effects.*

Whether to have your Shih Tzu neutered is a decision that you should make together with your veterinarian. Your veterinarian will advise you about the benefits and possible risks of neutering your pet and answer any questions you may have.

Identification Is Important

The very first thing you should do, as soon as possible after you bring your new companion home, is to be sure she is properly identified. If your Shih Tzu is ever lost or stolen, your chances of being reunited with her are very slim without proper identification. Ninety percent of all lost family pets are unidentifiable and 70 percent of these animals never return home. Annually, millions of lost American pets are euthanized because they are not identified and their owners cannot be located. Don't let your little lion dog become one of the statistics. Contact your veterinarian right away and schedule an appointment to have your Shih Tzu microchipped. You'll be glad you did.

Microchips

A microchip is a permanent and effective form of animal identification. A microchip is a microtransponder the size of a grain of rice that is implanted under the skin quickly and easily by injection. The microchip has a series of numbers unique to itself so that each animal has its own identification number. A handheld scanner (also called a decoder or reader) is used to read the identification number. Microchips are safe, permanent, and tamper-proof. The entire identification procedure (microchip implant or scanning) takes only a few seconds. Scanning is absolutely painless and accurate.

Once an animal has been implanted with a microchip, the following information is entered into a central computer registry: animal's identification number, a description of the animal, the owner's name,

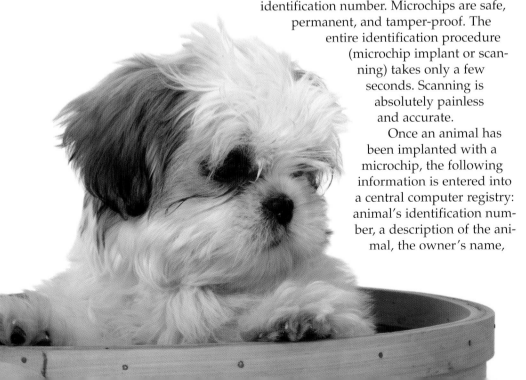

address, and telephone number, and an alternate contact in case the owner cannot be reached. It is the owner's responsibility to update the registry in the event of a change in information. An identification tag for the animal's collar also is provided, indicating the animal's identification number and the registry's telephone number.

Lost animals can be identified at animal shelters, humane societies, and veterinary offices. Once the animal's identification number is displayed, the central registry is contacted and the owner's information is released for contact.

Collars and Nametags

Collars and nametags are excellent forms of identification and they are easy and inexpensive. Many local pet stores offer nametag engraving. Collars and tags are easily visible and let others know your lost companion has a family. The obvious disadvantage of this type of identification is that if your Shih Tzu loses her collar or nametag, she will be without identification. Also, most Shih Tzu do not wear collars full-time.

Tattoos

Many veterinarians offer tattoo identification for dogs. Tattoos are considered a good form of identification because they are permanent. However, they are not a good identification alternative for Shih Tzu because it is difficult to tattoo many numbers on a Shih Tzu's inner thigh or belly, due to their small size. It is also difficult to see a tattoo because of the dog's long hair (the coat would have to be shaved to see the tattoo).

CAUTION

Register your Shih Tzu with the American Kennel Club Animal Recovery Database.

147

Tattoos can fade over time. They cannot be altered or "updated," so contact numbers that change, such as telephone numbers, are not good numbers to use. There are several tattoo registries, so it is often difficult for the finder to contact you. For all of these reasons, while tattoos are helpful, they should never be used alone as a source of animal identification.

Travel with Your Shih Tzu

Shih Tzu love to travel and a well-mannered Shih Tzu makes a wonderful ambassador for the breed. Whether you are on a long vacation or a short outing, your Shih Tzu traveling companion can make the trip all the more fun.

Here are a few tips to help make traveling with your Shih Tzu safe and enjoyable for everyone.

CAUTION

Do not give your Shih Tzu tranquilizers if you are traveling by air. Tranquilizers can cause death in dogs at flight altitudes. Even at ground level, tranquilization can hinder breathing if your pet is heavily sedated. Tranquilizers are especially risky for brachycephalic breeds like Shih Tzu.

- Train your Shih Tzu to a crate early in life so she will feel comfortable and secure inside it when you travel together.
- Make a few short practice trips, even if it's just driving around the block.
- Make sure your Shih Tzu is in excellent health and able to make the trip.
- Ask your veterinarian to examine your Shih Tzu and verify that all necessary vaccinations are up-to-date.
- Check with your veterinarian to know if any special medications for the trip are recommended, such as preventive heartworm medication or medication to prevent car sickness.
- Ask your veterinarian to refill any prescriptions that your Shih Tzu will need on the trip.
- Obtain a health certificate for your Shih Tzu within 10 days of out-of-state travel.
- Make hotel and airline reservations well in advance and advise you are traveling with a pet.
- Make a list of what you will need and pack in advance.

On the plane, your Shih Tzu may be small enough to fit comfortably under the seat in front of you in her crate. If she is not, she will be assigned a space in the cargo hold. Be sure to make advance reservations. With heightened airline security, not all airlines currently ship animals in cargo, so check with the airlines *before* you make reservations. Ask the airline

company what their specific requirements are so that you will be prepared *before* you arrive at the airport. Only a limited number of animals may travel on a given flight, either in the cabin or in the cargo hold, so make your reservation as early as you can.

If you are traveling by car or boat and your Shih Tzu is not used to them, she may get motion sickness. To reduce the likelihood that your Shih Tzu will be nauseous or sick, limit her food and water one to two hours before travel begins and, if possible, place her crate where she can see outside activities.

CHECKLIST

Your Shih Tzu's Travel Needs

- ✔ Crate
- ✔ Collar with identification tag and leash
- ✔ Dishes, food, water bottle, and bottled water
- ✔ Exercise pen with clips
- ✔ Sun shade cover and roll-up floor mat for exercise pen
- ✔ Medications

- ✔ First aid kit
- ✔ Toys and bedding from home
- ✔ Grooming supplies
- ✔ Clean-up equipment: pooper scooper, plastic bags, paper towels, and carpet cleaner
- ✔ Veterinary records and photo identification
- ✔ Copy of microchip identification

Resources

Kennel and Breed Clubs

American Kennel Club (AKC)
Registrations
5580 Centerview Drive
Raleigh, NC 27606-3390
(919) 233-9767
www.akc.org

American Shih Tzu Club, Inc.
www.shihtzu.org

Canadian Kennel Club
89 Skyway Avenue, Suite 100
Etobicoke,
Ontario, Canada
M9W6R4
(416) 675-5511

North American Dog Agility Council
P.O. Box 277
St. Maries, ID 83861
(208) 689-3803

States Kennel Club
1007 W. Pine Street
Hattieburg, MS 39401
(601) 583-8345

United Kennel Club (UKC)
100 East Kilgore Road
Kalamazoo, MI 49001-5598
(616) 343-9020

United States Dog Agility
Association
P.O. Box 850955
Richardson, TX 75085-8955
(972) 231-9700
Fax: (214) 503-0161
info@usdaa.com
www.usdaa.com

Health-Related Associations and Foundations

American Kennel Club Canine
Health Foundation
251 W. Garfield Road
Aurora, OH 44202
(216) 995-0806
akchf@aol.com

American Society for the Prevention
of Cruelty to Animals (ASPCA)
424 East 92nd Street
New York, NY 10128-6804
(212) 876-7700
www.aspca.org

American Veterinary Medical
Association (AVMA)
930 North Meacham Road
Schaumberg, IL 60173
www.avma.org

Association of Pet Dog Trainers
(APDT)
150 Executive Center Drive, Box 35
Greenville, SC 29615
(800) PET-DOGS
Fax: (864) 331-0767
information@apdt.com
www.apdt.com

Canine Eye Registration Foundation
(CERF)
South Campus Court, Building C
West Lafayette, IN 47907

Delta Society
289 Perimeter Road E.
Renton, WA 98055
(800) 869-6898
www.deltasociety@cis.compuserve.com

Dogs for the Deaf
10175 Wheeler Road
Central Point, OR 97502
(541) 826-9220
info@dogsforthedeaf.org
www.dogsforthedeaf.org

Hearing Dogs for Deaf People
The Training Centre
London Rd. (A40)
Lewknor, Oxon 0X95RY
England
011-44-1844-353-898
info@hearing-dogs.co.uk
www.hearing-dogs.co.uk

National Animal Poison Control
Center (NAPCC)
Animal Product Safety Service
1717 South Philo Road, Suite 36
Urbana, IL 61802
(888) 4ANI-HELP
(888) 426-4435
(900) 680-0000
(Consultation fees apply, call for
details)
www.napcc.aspca.org

National Education for Assistance
Dog Services
P.O. Box 213
West Boylston, MA 01583
(508) 422-9064
www.neads.org

Orthopedic Foundation for Animals
(OFA)
2300 Nifong Boulevard
Columbia, MO 65201
www.prodogs.com

San Francisco SPCA Hearing Dog
Program
2500 16th St.
San Francisco, CA 94103
(415) 554-3020
hearingdog@sfspca.org
www.sfspca.org

Therapy Dogs International
88 Bartley Road
Flanders, NJ 07836
(973) 252-9800
Fax: (973) 252-7171
tdi@gti.net
www.tdi-dog.org

Lost Pet Registries

The American Kennel Club (AKC)
AKC Companion Recovery
5580 Centerview Drive, Suite 250
Raleigh, NC 27606-3394
(800) 252-7894
E-mail: *found@akc.org*
www.akc.org/car.htm

AVID
PETtrac
3179 Hamner Avenue
Norco, CA 92860-9972
(800) 336-AVID
E-mail: *PETtrac@AvidID.com*
www.avidmicrochip.com

Home Again Microchip Service
(800) LONELY-ONE
www.homeagainpets.com

National Dog Registry (NDR)
P.O. Box 118
Woodstock, NY 12498-0116
(800) 637-3647

Petfinders
368 High Street
Athol, NY 12810
(800) 223-4747

Periodicals

The American Kennel Club Gazette
51 Madison Avenue
New York, NY 10010

Dog Fancy
Subscription Division
P.O. Box 53264
Boulder, CO 80323-3264
(303) 786-7306 / 666-8504
www.dogfancy.com

Dogs USA Annual
P.O. Box 55811
Boulder, CO 80322-5811
(303) 786-7652

Dog World
29 North Whacker Drive
Chicago, IL 60606
(312) 726-2802

Books

The Complete Dog Book, *Official Publication of the American Kennel Club.* New York, NY: Howell Book House, 1992.

Dadds, Audrey. *The Shih Tzu.* New York, NY: Howell Book House, 1976.

Dunbar, Ian. *The Essential Shih Tzu.* New York, NY: Howell Book House, 1999.

Joris, Victor. *The Complete Shih Tzu.* New York, NY: Howell Book House, 1994.

Sucher, Jaime. *Shih Tzu: A Complete Pet Owner's Manual.* Hauppauge, New York: Barron's Educational Series, Inc., 2000.

Vanderlip, Sharon. *The Shih Tzu Handbook.* Hauppauge, New York: Barron's Educational Series, Inc. 2004.

White, Jo Ann. *The Official Book of the Shih Tzu.* Neptune City, NJ: T.F.H. Publications, 1995.

Index

THE TEAM BEHIND THE *TRAINING YOUR DOG* DVD

Host **Nicole Wilde** is a certified Pet Dog Trainer and internationally recognized author and lecturer. Her books include *So You Want to be a Dog Trainer* and *Help for Your Fearful Dog* (Phantom Publishing). In addition to working with dogs, Nicole has been working with wolves and wolf hybrids for over fifteen years and is considered an expert in the field.

Host **Laura Bourhenne** is a Professional Member of the Association of Pet Dog Trainers, and holds a degree in Exotic Animal Training. She has trained many species of animals including several species of primates, birds of prey, and many more. Laura is striving to enrich the lives of pets by training and educating the people they live with.

Director **Leo Zahn** is an award winning director/cinematographer/editor of television commercials, movies, and documentaries. He has directed and edited more than a dozen instructional DVDs through the Picture Company, a subsidiary of Picture Palace, Inc., based in Los Angeles.